STUDENT NURSE
MAY...

BY ANNETTE BROWN

STUDENT NURSE MAY 1966

COPYRIGHT ANNETTE BROWN: 2014-04-12

ALL RIGHTS RESERVED

No part of this book may be reproduced in any form
By photocopying or any electronic or mechanical means,
Including information storage or retrieval systems, without
Permission in writing from the Copyright holder.

STUDENT NURSE MAY 1966

This book is about Student Nurse Training in the 1960's.
At the time Nursing was treated as a Vocation, and was very badly paid, with long hours of employment and very demanding work.
At the time of commencement of the training, the Labour Party under Harold Wilson was in Office. They were supposed to be the champions of working people, but they showed no care or interest in Nurses, and the gross exploitation of the Trainees and Qualified Nurses either. The Government were hypocrites who talked big, but did nothing to help us.
Managing on the Nurses training allowance was very difficult. Most Student Nurses were 'subbed' by their parents, but with my background there was no chance of this.
Being used to poverty at home, I was able to stick the training out. During my off-duty I would work for a London Agency's clients to earn extra money and this did make a big difference.

As far as I was concerned the training was three years of penury. A very hard time was experienced, and at an age when most teenagers are out and about and enjoying themselves, I was worn down with work, had no social life to speak of and lived a hand to mouth existence. In spite of this it was a very memorable and interesting time of my life. I met many lovely people and had incredible experiences. I got to see a whole panorama of humanity, and learned an amazing amount about people, their frailties and what hardship some had to endure.

Having had experience of such sick and ill people, it made one appreciate one's own good health. A lesson learned was that good health is a blessing from on high. You can't buy it and this was brought home many times when I nursed wealthy, private patients who had cancer or some other terminal disease, and in spite of paying out huge amounts of money they lost their lives.

Like rain, ill health can fall on all of us.

Doctors and Nurses both then and now do sterling work.

Most of them are indeed vocational and offer kind, caring and professional support for the sick and needy. I have the utmost respect for all Hospital Staff and am proud that I was once numbered amongst them.

This book is a follow up to 'The Most Hateful Child God Ever Put Breath Into'. By Annette Brown.

THE GREAT ESCAPE

After I left home in Cyprus it was with feelings of great happiness, joy and freedom as I finally escaped the clutches of my horrible parents Reg and Hilda. All my memories of 18 years of living with them were bad. There was serial abuse and brutality and I was the classic scapegoat in a cruel and oppressive relationship. I had been subject to regular beatings and hurt. Now I found myself forgetting. I simply buried the memories even though at a conscious level I detested my parents, somehow the separation made things OK and I could cope and in fact function extraordinarily well. What had happened never existed and my future would not be complicated by nerve wracking recall. I was full of optimism and never doubted my ability to get on and prosper.
There was a great future to be had somewhere and the plans I had were all win, win!

I returned to the UK on a RAF plane ahead of the Brown family as I had an interview for nurse training in London.
We arrived at Lyneham in Wiltshire and I needed the train to London so that I could get a connection to Bexley in Kent where my aunt Dot and uncle Bert lived and where I was to stay.

On the platform at Lyneham was a kiosk selling sweets and having broken into one of my pound notes for the train ticket, I bought a bar of Galaxy chocolate. It tasted good and I felt rich with the £25 I had in sterling. It was a goodly sum in 1965, but years later I realised it should have been more.
Each month I had handed my sister Susan £5 Cyprus, to save for this trip home and she had bought me five Premium Bonds with the money. The exchange rate was not equal and the Cyprus pound was worth almost £6 sterling and Susan must have pocketed the difference. Pretty sick, as she knew I was hard up and earned twice what I did anyway. It took many years later after a holiday to Cyprus for me to realise what she had done.
Reg and Hilda gave me no financial or other help with this journey and without these savings I would have been in a real mess.

The trip to Kent wasn't memorable but my aunt and uncle gave me a warm welcome and were always very kind to me.
I had decided to disconnect permanently with my parents but did not share this notion and just did not talk about them or what had happened.

As it turned out I did reconnect with Reg and Hilda and have regretted it to this very day.

It was November when I returned and I was 18 years old. My aunt lived in a small detached house and my cousin had to give up her room for me. She slept on a put-u-up with her parents and her tiny room with kiddy-sized furniture was mine. The Nursing interview was the following week and this was Friday so I spent the next few days settling in and presented my aunt and uncle with souvenirs of Cyprus. Foreign travel for holidays was the prerogative of only the wealthy in those days so anything overseas was regarded as exotic! Anyway they seemed pleased with the Greek style pottery given and I felt I had done the right thing.

I really did not know what to do. My main option to avoid going home was to get a live - in job somewhere and this meant being a Children's Nanny. I discussed this with my aunt and although did not tell her about life with Reg and Hilda she soon understood that I was not going back to them. She did not ask why and I didn't tell her!
Generously she said I could stay with her until I started Nursing and get myself a job in London. A lot of people in Bexley commuted to London daily for work and that included my uncle. It all seemed possible but as I did not have typing skills and only the Library work experience my choices were a bit limited. Still the Nursing interview was on Tuesday, and after that I would go to employment agencies to try and find paid work.

Westminster Hospital was a London teaching hospital for Medical Students, General Nurses and Children's Nurses. It was the only interview I booked so had nothing to compare it with. In fact it was very poor on Nurses welfare with lousy living accommodation and high charges for such. I didn't realise this until after I started my training and by then it was too late to do anything about it. I would have been much better off in a provincial hospital for the SRN (State Registered Nurse) training but at the time thought a London Teaching hospital was the summit of achievement and even when shown the crummy Nurses Home and told we could not use the hospital lift I had no idea what an impoverished lifestyle I would be taking on.
To qualify as a Registered Nurse took three years, and was mainly a 'Hands-on' training with a small allocation of Nursing School, and academic study. A training allowance was paid but it was very low, and would become a struggle to live on if no parental support was

forthcoming. I had very little idea what sort of future this would be, and it was a case of travelling in hope. The grinding poverty was also an unknown, but probably this was just as well. Full of hope and optimism, it was essential to get some sort of professional qualification, and Nursing ticked a lot of boxes.

My interview was with the Matron- One Lavinia Young. Whilst sitting waiting to see her there was a photo album with pictures of hospital staff who had operated on the previous King for lung cancer. The Hospital seemed proud of this and ignored the fact that their royal patient had not survived his treatment. I studied the pictures of white coated doctors and fussily garbed and hatted nurses and felt a little alienated as was no Royalist and this grovelling and Royalty worship was offensive to me.
I went into my interview with the Matron and was asked why I wanted to do nursing. "Well to help people of course"-plus I added the interest in the clinical side and a desire to know more about disease and anatomy.
I must have said the right things as was told I would be starting in the following May with older girls. Little did I know that there was such a shortage of nurses and the cheap labour provided by students that even if I had two heads and one arm I would have been accepted. Unasked the Matron described two Nanny jobs she had that I could get experience for nursing with. The pay was terrible. About £3 per week so I politely declined these pathetic job offers and felt I could do a lot better finding my own job in London. In fact these Nanny jobs would have been good preparation for nursing with little money and long, exhausting hours. Gross exploitation all round!
At the time I had no idea of the Student Nurse lifestyle and what a testing time it would be. I was enthusiastic and felt that becoming an SRN was the key to the door and would give many golden opportunities. This was a correct assumption, but the journey there was one, long, hard slog.
I left the interview jubilant. A major goal was achieved in the Nursing offer. I now needed to find a job to support myself and remain living with my aunt and uncle.
That very day before I went home I got a bus to Oxford Street and visited a couple of employment agencies.

1 Annette Brown aged 18 years. Passport photograph.

A JOB IS FOUND AND WHAT A JOB TOO!

My lack of typing and secretarial skills was a problem. One woman who interviewed me was incredibly rude and more or less said I was unemployable and criticised my appearance. She was so bitchy I wondered if anyone ever got a job from her ?
The next Agency had a mumsy lady doing the interview and she decided there was a future for me as a Credit Controller and arranged an interview for later in the week. The pay seemed OK so felt happy and successful as I went to Charing Cross station and got the train back to Bexley.
My aunt had a broadsheet newspaper each day and there were always jobs advertised. One caught my eye. It was for a 'City Librarian' for a Sunday paper. I immediately phoned and was asked to put my application in writing which I did at once and posted it.
Two days later I was back in London for my job interview as Credit Controller.
I had trouble finding the place and spent some cash on a taxi to get there on time. It was a weird set up and after an interview and brief explanation about what the job entailed I was shown my desk in the office.
This was high rise and very ancient. There were about six other staff working on similar desks and each had a phone. No doubt for ringing debtors.
The Boss who interviewed me was a real creep. He was in his thirties and an obvious sexual predator. His attitude made me feel very uncomfortable and working in his firm would be a truly Dickensian experience complete with his horrible behaviour. In the end I felt I was lucky to leave with my clothes on but was offered the job which at £12 per week was much better than the Nanny jobs. I didn't accept as was hoping for the Newspaper job. The very next day brought a letter and offer of an interview for it.
Once again a few days later I set out for London. This time the City, where the offices were situated. Again having got lost, had to get a taxi. My money was going fast.
I found the office location, and met the Editor's secretary. She was very sweet and we chatted and laughed for ages before I met the Chief. The interview was brief and informal. I felt more than adequate for the job which appeared to be that of a filing clerk.
Home back in Bexley there was an anxious wait for the post to arrive. There were phone calls from the Agency who found me the Credit job and I got Aunty Dot to take the calls and say I was out. These calls increased to about four a day and my aunt began to get annoyed.
Another couple of days passed and a letter arrived from the Sunday Newspaper miraculously offering me the job of City Librarian. I was overjoyed and pranced about cheering and doing hi fives. My aunt was amused but said that we needed to deal with the phone calls from the agency!
I rang the Newspaper and spoke to the Editor and accepted the job. I would only be there six months because of the Nursing but kept this information to myself. I was very selfish like most teenagers and left my poor aunt to sort out the Agency asking her to say I had left London for the country. The woman was very persistent and carried on ringing for many more days. Probably the horrible, lecherous Boss who had interviewed me was pressuring her and decided to hide behind my aunt.
With hindsight it was a blessing that I did not need to work for such a man..
The Newspaper paid well. Union rates and this was to be £13 per week which was good money. Dot only wanted £2.50 for my board and keep so It was a good opportunity to get a nest egg for nursing.
My social life in Bexley took off. My cousin Carolyn who was a year older than me lived close by and we would go out together meeting her friends. On top of that a neighbour's son

introduced himself and had thought that I was the family's Au-Pair. He had a green sports car and I started to see him on a regular basis.

Also there was contact with an army captain called Peter from Cyprus.. He was in the UK and we had been corresponding. I had a big crush on him and had high hopes for our future relationship. He was incredibly handsome, and of romantic Russian parentage.

Peter took me out for one night in London and then dumped me. I was upset about this at the time as I never heard from him again. He was 10 years older than me and obsessed with the army and sport so I was well shot of him, but at the time felt very hurt. The other opportunities more than made up for this abandonment and I was having a really good time.

I started my job and as there was no one to show me the ropes had to work out what was required. Each day Newspaper copies x 4 arrived on my desk and they had to be scanned for City news done by our journalists and cut out the information and paste it into company files with the date added. There were dozens of files and I also had to include company reports and stock advice letters. I found the Finance boring but it was a good and easy job and I enjoyed it. The other staff were very nice and I shared my office with a part- time secretary who was on a very cushy number. It was a spacious and very comfortable office and I was lucky to be on my own there for much of the time. The only downside was joining the Union plus a couple of journalists who would come in complaining that some small piece they had written had been missed. If the later had occurred it was necessary to telephone for extra copies of the Newspaper to retrieve the two lines or so of printed word! It was important to co-operate even though their demands were petty and irritating.

In those days you had to join the Union or no job. It was called NATSOPA and it was pretty obvious people were afraid to fall foul of it and lose their jobs. Occasionally there was compulsory attendance at a meeting where their irritating brand of Communism was preached. The only solution to this unpleasant unionisation was to keep your head down, go along with them and hopefully keep your job. On top of that there were salary deductions for the Union and a percentage of this went to fund the Labour Party. I am not a Socialist in any shape or form and found this 'Closed Shop' sickening.

I became a firm friend of the Editor's secretary Brenda, and we would go out for meals after work. She told me that there had been over 100 applications for my job. Many from highly trained Librarians. It was my friendship with her that earned me the job as she admitted to persuading the Editor to give it to me.

Because we were good friends I got involved with helping at Finance parties given for Business leaders and Journalists. These parties did not involve any food and were just a major booze up. Most of the Journalists had an obvious drink problem and as the whiskey and wine flowed free they became merrier and drunker. It was all highly entertaining. There was a lot of power in the Newspaper industry and I recall one sub-Editor ringing a Company Secretary and asking him if he knew his Company had just been taken over on a share buy out. I think the receiver of this call collapsed in shock! The City staff were privy to a lot of confidential information and were happy to use this for their own ends. They worked sporadically and a lot of the job involved high power networking and chatting on the phone. Mostly they were good fun. I think a lot of people would be surprised at how left -wing some of the Journalists were, working for a right -wing newspaper.

A lot of the younger ones in particular seemed obsessive, insular and miserable.

One day after one of the booze parties a middle- aged journalists offered me a lift home. He lived in Kent too, but it was out of his way. Drink driving was no bother then and he had a skinful when we set off. I felt it was a bit of a nuisance to him but he did have a purpose in

offering me the lift. He began to discuss The Editor and Brenda and wanted to know if they were having an affair?
I really didn't know but thought not as Brenda was not that sort of person. The questions were relentless and it became very annoying. Eventually we arrived home and I could not get out of the car quick enough. I really felt used and was cross that the generous lift was offered on the basis that my Boss and friend were slandered!
However this was typical behaviour and I was sure that any info I gave would be shared all round the Newspaper.

The secretary who shared my spacious office was called Lisa and never stopped talking about her fiancé and forthcoming marriage. She had a really easy job and worked afternoons for four hours or so doing mainly audio typing. She seldom had more than five letters to do and would talk non-stop. I liked her but found her obsessive engagement fixation boring. In the February she arrived at the office one day red eyed and sniffing. It seemed that the fiancé had pulled out of the wedding and all her plans were in ruins. She was totally devastated and spent the afternoon crying all over the letters she typed up. It was very sad and there was nothing much you could say to comfort her. She told me she had a lot of goods in her ' bottom drawer' and when she heard that my sister was getting married insisted I bought two blankets off her as a wedding gift. There really was no choice . They were forced on me and not wanting to upset her further I agreed to take them.

RECONNECTING WITH REG AND HILDA

Hilda and Reg and my sisters had returned from Cyprus and were living in Fradley near Lichfield in RAF married quarters for Officers. I had not been in touch with them and had no intention of so doing. However a wedding invitation arrived in January for Susan's wedding to Alex on the 2nd April. Aunty Dot intended to go and there was an assumption I would go with them. It was a very difficult situation and really there was no way of refusing to go, as did not want to discuss my horrible life and memories with this nice aunty.

I rang up Joanne who was still in Bristol. The first thing she said to me was that I sounded "terribly posh".
This was really annoying, and then she dropped her bombshell. Not only had she left her Commercial Art course at the West of England College but she was going out with a lorry driver who had left his wife and three kids to be with her. She was living with him and was working at her aunts Arty shop. She was a really pretty and attractive girl who could have snapped her fingers and had any man. Why had she done this? I was horrified at the information and decided the abandoned kids she was responsible for were a barrier to our future friendship. I never rang her again and that was the end of the relationship. Although common nowadays that sort of situation was rare in the 1960's and it was totally sickening.

I also met up with another friend from Bristol. Jillian ,who had moved to London with her family.

That did not turn out well either. Her family were very odd, and she was man mad. We visited the Hammersmith Palais for dances at night but within minutes of going there she would find some man to dance with and disappear for the evening. I was left on my own and was annoyed by repulsive would be suitors and eventually had to go home alone. She would ring me at work the next day and according to her was practically engaged to the man from the dance hall. These relationships lasted one date usually and then the guy would disappear. Back we would go to Hammersmith and after a few sessions I contrived to avoid her.
The root of this behaviour was to escape her family and later I heard she had moved out of home into a shared house to continue her manhunt which eventually was successful.

The other friend I connected with was Jennifer from Cyprus who still had her BMW car. Initially she and her parents were living in a Service Flat in Bayswater but after a bit they went into a new build house in Ealing.
I visited her there and realised that the family were quite wealthy as the furnishings and home were very luxurious and Jennifer had a privileged lifestyle.
One day Jennifer invited me to meet with her cousin in Cambridge who was newly married. We drove there in the BMW and arrived at a very pretty thatched cottage for Sunday lunch. This turned out to be badly cooked roast duck but it was a generous invitation and the outing much enjoyed. The cousin told me that the house they had was the previous home of Frank Whittle the Jet engine inventor and I was most impressed as was an admirer of this iconic engineer

Susan's wedding loomed large. My two younger sisters were to be bridesmaids, but no invitation or communication came to me and I really did not want to go to the event.
Aunty Dot assumed we would all be going together in the family car. My young cousins were not invited and were to spend the day with a relative.
In March, Dot and I visited a somewhat Matronly ladies dress shop in Bexley village to purchase wedding outfits. I chose a cream silk two piece suit which was quite expensive. It was expected that the weather in April would be warm and what a mistake that was; time flew and not only was the wedding fast approaching but my Nurse training.
I was going to have to tell Brenda and the Editor that I was leaving and give notice and felt a bit embarrassed as I had obviously used them as 'gap' employment and they had always been very kind to me. I had taken advantage of them and only worked for six months and was now leaving.
 At the time I had a big social life with lots of friends and was in a really good place. There was no idea then that it would all go with the Nursing and I might as well have taken Holy orders and enter a Nunnery as this was the end result.
Geoff the boyfriend with the sports car was becoming a pest. He was OK but very possessive and had friends I did not like. He was also over-sexed, but aunty Dot liked him. He worked as a buyer at Smithfield meat market and would frequently greet me on our dates with bloody lumps of meat. Always prized cuts and my aunt got the benefit of these gifts. I was not a meat lover and would have preferred chocolates if gifts were coming my way - but no, it was gory piles of meat.
At the weekends Geoff would take me out into the Kent countryside. Usually we would end up in Pubs and Geoff would buy drinks. In Cyprus the favourite tipple was a Tom Collins cocktail and I always asked for one of these. After a few weeks Geoff got a bit annoyed and said the cocktail was very expensive and what else did I like. He suggested cider which was loved so we did a transfer and Geoff was happy. One day we went to a Pub in Tonbridge in Kent and there was Scrumpy on sale made by the Pub. I had several glasses of this nectar and ended up legless with Geoff having to carry me to the car to get home. Aunt Dot was not

impressed when she saw me and the state I was in! However nothing was said as at the next visit Geoff brought along a large pack of fillet steak.

Another lad turned up to ask out the 'Au-Pair', this time to a party. Somehow Geoff found out and the trip was vetoed. I should have gone as our relationship had no future anyway.

One night on a Saturday staying home alone while Dot and family went out for the evening, something useful was done for Aunty Dot.

I felt nervous at being alone and the Eurovision Song Contest was on the T V so had that on extremely loud. The next day we heard that all the neighbour's houses had been broken into and burgled so my noisy presence had saved the day. I was classed as a useful hero and wallowed in the praise!

SUSAN'S WEDDING IS CELEBRATED

Susan's wedding day was here and Aunty Dot, Uncle Bert and myself all went to Lichfield for the event, which was being celebrated in Fradley church followed by a reception and meal in a large, expensive Hotel in the City centre.

As we arrived at the church I spotted my younger two sisters waiting for the bride clad in blue, glistening, tube like dresses. They were far from flattering and in fact looked downright ugly. I spotted Hilda and Reg inside the church. Hilda wore a very plain outfit and silly hat. Reg was in his RAF uniform as were many of the other men present. Both of them contrived to ignore me but it was difficult as they had to show some regard for Dot and Bert.

It was a freezing cold day and the summer silk suit being worn was a really bad choice for by the time we left the church it was snowing.

Susan wore a classic white gown that was far more attractive than the blue tubes her bridesmaids sported. She really looked good on the day with a smart hairdo, and well applied makeup. Alex must have thought he'd done well with such a prize. After the ceremony and as we left the church Alex's brother Officers, formed a sword archway for the bride and groom to walk under. This was followed by photographs but not many as the snow was getting heavier and we all made a dash for the Hotel.

Once inside the hotel it was apparent that most of the guests were from Alex's Squadron, and they were all very thirsty. The till on the bar was on Reg's tab and was ringing non-stop as pints of beer, warming brandies and all manner of expensive drinks were sluiced down. The free bar was a dream come true for the Squadron and they pitched in with gusto.

The meal was not memorable but done to high standards. Reg and Hilda paid for everything and Hilda looked stressed out and unhappy as she observed the Squadron guzzling down her money! There was nothing to be done so my tight fisted parents had to put on a brave face.

I was totally ignored by Susan, Alex and Hilda and Reg. Treated like a pariah and made to feel most unwelcome. At the time it was not obvious, but Susan ensured that I was excluded from all the family photographs, so I have no visual record of this occasion. The gift blankets had been wrapped up and were left with other presents. Due to the extreme cold and icy road conditions we left early and motored back to Kent.

I really wished not to have gone. Maxine and Margaret had chatted but did not seem happy with their role and later said they hated the dresses they were forced to wear and like everyone else were frozen to the bone. So that was one hurdle over and done with. Another unpleasant, family memory.

Now I had to give notice to the Newspaper and firstly confided in Brenda who asked me to put this in writing and give a month. The Nursing started on 9th May 1966, and time was running out. The Editor was very nice about it all and supportive about the career choice. Not

only that but he said that he, Brenda and I would go for a farewell lunch before I left and I could select any restaurant that I liked. This was typical of the kindness shown in this job and I chose to go to the Savoy hotel which I had heard a lot about.
We went about a week before I left and the cream silk suit got another airing. It was a fabulous meal and a memorable occasion for which I was very grateful. It had been a privilege to work on the newspaper with such lovely people. I knew that they would be much missed.

Suddenly I was packing my case and stashing all the goodies that had been acquired during the Bexley stay. I had a lot of new clothes, a smart wristwatch, a Nurses fob watch, a transistor radio and a tape recorder. I had also been to the bookshop and purchased a Nurses Textbook and dictionary. After saying my goodbyes to my aunt and family, Dot presented me with a silver charm bracelet as a memento and asked me to keep in touch. I was very grateful to her and said so over and over. Another Aunt Joan turned up as well to see me off and it felt really sad to be leaving them all. However Dot's house was a bit cramped with me in it and am sure they were relieved to see me go.

THE NURSE TRAINING COMMENCES

The Preliminary Training School for student Nurses was located in Vincent Square close to the Westminster Hospital. We were housed in a converted hotel in Craven Hill Gardens, Bayswater and bussed to the school every day for eight weeks.
On arrival I was shown my room and on the bed waiting for me was a Nurses Uniform. Lots of girls had arrived and were buzzing round, some trying on the dresses and aprons. After unpacking I decided to try on the uniform. We had previously sent in our measurements. Horrors- it was much too tight. Panic set in, but the girl next door Sarah was bemoaning the fact that her own uniform was too big so we did a swop and the problem was solved. There was a blue denim dress that fell to mid- knee and a same fabric belt, white detachable collar and Apron . There were two cloaks, both in navy –blue wool. A short one lined in red and a long, heavy one for outside wear. A small, very old fashioned bonnet was given to wear with the long cloak. A Paper nurses hat in plain white was provided and this was the PTS gear as we were called with which we were to venture onto the wards and out in the public domain.

I had seen Sarah arrive out the window. Her parents brought her in the family Rolls-Royce and she told me that her dad was a Consultant doctor and her mum an ex- Nurse. They had both met and trained at the Westminster and so it was evocative that their only child was now following in their footsteps. Things did not really work out for Sarah , as she did meet her husband at the hospital but it was an Italian Porter as opposed to a doctor. I think when she married him it must have been a bit of a let- down for the parents. Still, as long as she was happy what more could be said?
I met other girls all nervous but chatty and as we were roomed alphabetically made friends with a B and C!
The hotel was very pleasant, warm and comfortable. A far cry from the Nurses home we entered after the first six weeks, but with so much comfort I really felt I had fallen on my feet.
Somehow Reg had got my new Nursing address and sent me a letter, hand -written endorsing the Nurse training which amazed me. I don't think Hilda knew about this letter or would have

banned it. I would have appreciated a few quid with the letter, but as usual there was nothing. Reg worshipped education and later I heard that the family had bet that I would not do the Nursing but stay in the Newspaper job. Obviously it had shocked Reg enough to take pen to paper.

Monday came and all 65 of us trainee Nurses piled onto a bus wearing pristine new uniforms and were taken to the Wolfson School Of Nursing, the Hospital state- of- the- art training centre. We knew that we were green and ignorant but we discovered that some of our number had been cadets in a Northern hospital and had a lot of Ward experience.

The first lesson we had was on ethics. Confidentiality was essential and service above self. We were told how lucky we were to be training at such a splendid hospital and would be supervised in our work and as well as going on the wards we would have regular weeks in the training school as well as 'on the job' instruction.

After this introduction we had buns and coffee. It all seemed very civilised.

The Nurse Tutors were a varied bunch and ranged from the bossy Matron like, to the thoughtful intellectual. There was no mentoring in those days, but I developed a good rapport with a Sister Simpson, and she was helpful and supportive over my training time.

Our first lesson was how to make a hospital bed. This involved making perfect corners and the use of a 'Drawsheet'. This was a strip of sheet that could be pulled to and fro across the bed to keep the patient cool and fresh. In fact it's main use was to soak up pee from the incontinent! This was a a good device for saving excessive use of newly laundered sheets and must have saved the hospital quite a lot of money.

There was a bed rest to stack pillows on. We were taught how to lift and move patients and practiced on each other, causing loads of giggles and hilarity. How to change a bed with the patient in it and how to preserve the patients modesty at all costs .

We were instructed on how to supply a bedpan and help the patient on and off it.

Other things we were shown was 'oral toilet' how to clean false choppers and the mouths of the very weak or unconscious. A Bedbath,and the treatment of Pressure areas. This latter was massage to the small of the back, heels and elbows. It was ritualistic and frequently done on patients who did not need it. It was very time consuming and the rubbing of skin in such a vigorous manner is now thought to have caused pressure sores rather than prevented them. I hated pressure areas and must have done hundreds of them in the next three years of the training.

Bed baths were similarly done on people who were quite capable of washing themselves. Patients were babied and treated as objects. Bed bathing was very long winded and took up hours of our time.

In the school this procedure was given a high priority with numerous towels and wash cloths being used. Patients became Demi-gods once in a hospital bed and it was made very clear to us that we were subordinate in every way.

One useful and memorable happening was to make a visit to the Hospital for Tropical Disease to learn about bacteria and communicable disease.

The first thing we did was to be given an Agar Plate each and were each told to press our hand onto it. This we did and the plates were sent off for culture. We then had lectures on the need for hygiene in our work and the consequences to patients by neglecting basics like hand washing and wearing clean aprons. We were told how in old times Midwives would visit to deliver babies wearing filthy, blood stained clothes to prove their experience and with these and their dirty hands and nails caused death with a newly delivered mother contracting puerperal fever. Short finger nails were essential. Not only did long nails contain filth, but we could scratch vulnerable patients when lifting and moving them. We were told about 'Barrier

Nursing', and how this was used to protect Nurse and patient against the spread of disease. The rules of the Operating Theatre were explained and because micro-organisms are always in the air around us we were told how difficult it was to avoid infection in open surgical wounds. The history of hygiene was discussed and we learned about how Lister was the first to heal Compound (open) Fractures.

It was all very interesting and a vital part of our understanding for the need to keep things clean at all costs.

When we returned to the Tropical Disease Hospital the following week we got our Agar plates back, with a report on the bacteria found on our unwashed hands. We were shocked to learn that we carried Diptheria, Gas Gangrene, Polio, Measles and many nasty Pathogens. It was a real wake-up call and we all took to enthusiastic hand washing, wore our nails short, and hair tied well back.

Over the three years training as part of an audit on what we had achieved we were given Yellow Books (see glossary) containing all the practices Nurses should know and do. All these were achieved under the watchful eye of a ward sister and they were ticked and signed off. We were presented with these books at the commencement of our training and they composed a part of our final examinations. We had to take them with us and the ward staff would check out what new thing we needed to do.

We learned how to test urine specimens and when to report abnormalities. How to fill in the notes of a patient with results, and how to check a pulse, respiratory rate and body temperature. We also learned how to use a sphygmomanometer to take blood pressure readings, and what the normal range was.

As the six weeks in PTS progressed it became more and more obvious that we were very low down in the hospital hierarchy and had an awful lot to learn. I think most of us were nervous of starting work proper, and began to wonder what we had let ourselves in for. We had been instructed in basic Nursing. Work horses and cheap labour for the hospital. We failed to see or understand the gross exploitation which was perhaps just as well.

We had every weekend free in PTS and managed to see Brenda, Geoff and Jennifer at various times but somehow it seemed as if a door was closing on the non-hospital world. I became polarised and mixed almost exclusively with other nurses. One thing that happened was I began to grossly overeat.

I'd always had a tendency to be plump and really watched my diet but here in the PTS started to stuff myself. Initially it was with tubs of cream cheese but this worsened to peanuts, chocolate and big helpings at mealtimes. I started to balloon in my weight and this did not auger well for the strenuous physical demands of running round the wards! My weight was to become a bad problem throughout my training and over the three years I gained about 70 pounds- a total disaster.

The PTS was nearing the end of its eight weeks duration and lists appeared telling us which wards we were to be posted to and which Nurses Home we would be housed in. I was to go to the ENT Ward and the Queen Mary Nurses Home opposite the hospital. It was quite exciting and everyone was discussing the placements and eagerly anticipating the new life.

We had to wait a month to get our wages and the hospital opened bank accounts for us all. I got rather short of cash after four weeks not having saved much. When my pay slip arrived there was only £12 for the whole month and such a downward financial adjustment came hard. £3 per week did not go far and unlike my friends there were no generous cheques from home. This was the beginning of three years of grinding poverty. The training allowance was very low but we were charged more than half of it for our board and keep, and as we needed to supply black stockings and shoes plus chemist and outings the money was totally inadequate. It was known that Nursing was exploitive but I had not realised how bad things were. The money shut down everything that I had become used to and the Nursing became reclusive and a life of penury. Much later in my training I learned to generate more cash but initially finances were very tight indeed.

What made matters worse was that my two best Nurse friends Chris and Bau were both from wealthy, generous families and I could never keep up with them. They always had nice things and plenty of cash for the cinema etc but I frequently had to opt out of trips as I simply could not afford them and refused to scrounge or be subsidised. Money or lack of it became a worry that lasted for the full time of the training commitment. About a year after I finished my training there was an investigation into Nurses pay. There was an attitude that Nursing was a vocation and did not need paying. After a national report wages were increased but at the same time food had to be paid for and this did not resolve the problem as new areas of hardship and deprivation emerged. Nowadays trainee Nurses are paid a bursary so it is still a free training as opposed to most professional courses, but I gather the money remains poor and managing a struggle.

2 Fellow Nursing Students. Annette is in the top row, on left at end.

LOW STANDARD ACCOMMODATION

Several Nurses left after the PTS period. They realised that Nursing wasn't for them. About 60 of us were left
And now we had to move away from Bayswater and enter the Nurses Home in SW1.
What a dump it was. Horrible, faded, chintz curtains, linoleum on the floor. One cupboard and no plug sockets so I could not play my tape recorder any more. The room was small and overlooked the garbage courtyard and the heating generators droned loudly night and day. I don't think a prison cell would have been much worse- in fact from what I've heard Open Prison accommodation is vastly superior. The bathroom was communal but there was always lashings of hot water, so we Nurses could keep ourselves clean and fresh.
Our meals were served in a huge downstairs dining room, and you could eat all day long if you wanted to as the kitchen catered on a 24 hours basis for all the shifts . The food was

institutional but quite good enough for me to overeat and get fatter than ever. However it wasn't at all homely and compared to most other hospitals was a very low standard.
There was little consideration for the welfare of the Nurses and we new students got the lowest rating of all.
We were work fodder and paid at the net rate of about 8 pence an hour. Whilst possibly justifiable for newcomers it was appalling that in my third year of training with a lot of responsibility this pathetic stipend was still all that was paid.

I visited the ENT ward and got my shift rota. It was long days of 6.45am to 3.30pm or 1pm to 9pm. No night duty at first and I was asked to report on the ward early the next day. 7 or 8 days were worked on the trot and then one day off or so was given. Weekends off came every four or five weeks so you could whistle goodbye to a social life for good. Friends and family became a distant memory as the Hospital world swallowed you up. Anyone who has spent time in hospital knows it operates in its own time zone and is out of touch with ordinary life. The long hours and chronic tiredness soon turned me into a work drone with little else of note in my life. Some of the other nurses fared better and managed boyfriends and a social life beyond the Hospital.
They juggled shifts and always wanted 'Earlies' so they could keep their evenings free. I liked the 1-9pm shift because it allowed me a good lie in bed in the mornings and the ghastly Bedbaths for patients were done by the morning staff. I swopped my 'Earlies' many times for a 1-9pm shift and became very popular with other staff as was always willing.

On the 30th July I was out in London and saw the huge crowds of Football fans. England had won the World Cup and these fans were elated. Cheering, waving their arms and totally delighted. This was all observed but somehow even this important event of the 1960's failed to register. It was like nursing was a parallel dimension and everyday life had become meaningless.

Sometimes I wonder why I chose Nursing? I do not think I had a vocation for it at all and was not a very kind and caring person. It was a means to an end for me and one option that was considered with the SRN was to join one of the Military Nursing services. In the RAF if I trained in the service I would become a sergeant on qualification but entry from a civilian training conferred immediate officer status with the high pay and perks and this was a goal. There were loads of advertisements in the Nursing Press at that time for all sorts of opportunities and I felt that the sky really was the limit. Just three years to go!!

My first day on the Ward arrived. Dressed up in my Nurses uniform and feeling a complete fraud I arrived at 6.45am for the shift. There was plenty of work that morning. It was a Monday and surgery day for many of the patients. It was the ENT Ward (Ear, nose and throat) and although we had a couple of Bedbaths to do it was mostly prepping patients for surgery. I was sent to the men's wing on the Ward and one of them asked me for a Bottle! I stupidly thought he meant a hot-water bottle but on my way to the Sluice to search for one it suddenly dawned on me that he meant a male urinal bottle so having grabbed one, it was duly delivered. I realised if other Nurses had known of this gaffe I would have been a laughing stock.
I was closely supervised by the Staff Nurse who showed me the ropes and I shadowed her all day. I watched her give the pre-meds (relaxing shots prior to surgery) and was told to make up post-operative beds to receive the patients when they returned from the operating theatre. We had learned to make these beds in PTS, and as well as this we needed to put out a sick

bowl, chart for recording PTR (pulse, temperature and respiration)and a sphygmomanometer for blood pressure.

I watched as woozy post-anaesthetic patients were trollied back from theatre and helped lift them into bed. Most of the operations were for SMR (sub-mucous resection for severe rhinitis) and Nasal Polypectomy for similar reasons. Nasty conditions that made people's lives a misery.

Many of the patients became violently sick as they came round and it was my job to support them and catch in a bowl what was frequently bloody vomit. I soon began to feel sick myself but had to overcome this and clear up, settle the patient and then move on to the next one. I also had to do readings to ensure that a good recovery was taking place and there was no excessive post-operative bleeding.

We had to report any worries to a senior staff and to start with I was full of concern about everything. My other job with the newly operated on patients was to change their nasal bolsters. These were dressings tied under the nose to catch blood and serum. When they started to look soiled I had to remove them and supply a fresh one. It was a busy time especially if we had a major surgery case. To begin with I was only asked to help with the less serious cases where a quick and uneventful recovery was anticipated. Later I would be involved in assisting with very seriously ill patients but my first day although stressful passed without incident and though I didn't fancy my lunch after the gory sights nothing went amiss and I ended my shift at 3.30pm!

The Ward sister was called Sister McLeod and she was strict but fair. She was in her late forties and had a motherly attitude towards junior staff and was very supporting.

I soon got into a routine on the ENT and was taught a lot of new things. There were two wards each with about 20 beds in, plus private rooms in a corridor outside the wings. Most patients were in the general ward, either the women's or men's . The private rooms were for the very sick or dying, or for patients who paid for what was described as an 'Amenity bed'. There was a laundry room, treatment room, sluice and the Office. It was well organized and a self-contained unit.

At the start of each shift clad in a crisp, new apron we would crowd into the Sister's Office for a report. This was read from a book which had details of all the patients, their needs and treatments. Such things as Nursing care, X-rays , enemas, dressings and extra drugs were listed as well as basics like the Bedbaths and pressure areas. Malnourished or frail patients were ordered 'Complan' three or so times a day which was a nourishing drink. All this was written in the book and we had to refer to this throughout our time on duty, ticking off tasks as they were completed.

At that time modernisation of equipment and dressings was in process. Dressings and instruments were being sterilised by radiation or autoclave (high pressure steam) but we still had a boiler in our Duty room where we boiled up surgical instruments, kidney bowls and gallipots-all needed for wound dressings. There were also stainless steel trolleys that were used to do dressings and these had to be laid out in a specific manner and wheeled to the patient's bed as needed. When the treatment was over back they went and any instruments were cleaned and boiled for a minimum of 20 minutes and the trolleys swabbed with disinfectant. It was time consuming and modern nurses get small dressing packs on trays to take to the bedside and many instruments are plastic disposables.

The Duty room had a fridge for storing blood and some Drugs like insulin, plus there was a cupboard with the DDA's (Dangerous Drugs Act) such as Morphine and Pethidine. If one of these drugs was given two nurses had to check and sign to prevent theft and misuse.

All this had to be learned.

At the time if a patient was discharged we had to strip the bed, remove a plastic cover from the mattress and clean the bed and locker with disinfectant. A new plastic cover was put on the mattress and the bed made up with fresh linen and blankets. Sometimes a dozen or so patients were discharged and sorting the beds kept us very busy.

As is usual on any Hospital Ward there were always plenty of old people occupying the beds. I was not very sympathetic to them. They needed a lot of care, heaving off and on bedpans and often spoon feeding at mealtimes. Push fluids would say the report book which meant putting a cup of tea or Complan in a spouted cup and ages spent trying to get the patient to take it. Often these old people had given up and we were forcing them to carry on with this care. They would dribble and spit, and it was really very time consuming and often pointless.
One old lady came into the Ward and she was in a very poor condition of self- neglect, dehydration and general frailty. I had to admit her and found taking her blood pressure very difficult, and must have given pain as I had about eight goes. She was not very clean and her hair was wild and tangled.
Sister McLeod got involved in the admission process and pulled out the lady's false teeth, placed them in a bowl and told me to go and clean them.
They were in revolting condition. Covered in decaying food and other gunge (generic medical term for any disgusting substance). I did not want to handle them and found a cleaning brush and poured boiling water on them and swished them round in the bowl.
The teeth disintegrated and lay in pieces in the bowl. I really did not know what to do. Obviously my cleaning was too rough and now the dentures were ruined. I returned the set to the patient's locker and put the remains in a cardboard sputum box. The poor lady passed that night so loss of her teeth did not cause a problem, but it taught me to be careful with false teeth from then on.
We had a few patients in for extraction of impacted Wisdom teeth. Often they were medical students or Nurses and it was a nasty, messy procedure. Afterwards they would be sick from the anaesthetic, be oozing blood from the tooth sockets and experience a lot of pain as the Surgeons were rough. I realised that medical students were not exalted beings, but pretty much like other young people and just as vulnerable.
We also had adults having tonsillectomies and this operation was considered high risk due to the chance of haemorrhage after. The tonsil tissue was cut out, but not cauterised, and sometimes bleeding would take place and was swallowed. In this way a lot of blood could be lost and not detected. We had to take regular pulse and blood pressure readings in the post-operative period for a few hours to try and detect such a happening. Fortunately there were no problems with our patients, but this operation had fallen out of favour for children due to high mortality rates.

I had a rather unpleasant experience on this ward. We had a patient in who had been in a German POW camp. He had mental health issues stemming from this and was paranoid. He decided that because I had blonde hair I was a German and started shouting at me to keep away from him etc. I had no psychiatric experience and just tried to avoid him, but every time I came on the ward he would get abusive and it was embarrassing. I'm pleased to say that I had a couple of days off and when I came back he had gone. Sister McLeod had me in the office and explained his problems and said I had dealt with it very well and it was likely that he would have difficulties all over. I was glad he had gone and did not meet anything similar until towards the end of my training.

Another thing that upset me on this Ward was a poor man who came all the way from Cornwall for treatment of Maxilliary cancer. This was a malignancy of the jaw bone and really little could be done. However the surgeons decided to operate and do extensive surgery. This poor man was taken to the operating theatre and subjected to an 8 hours ordeal.

When he returned to the Ward he had a dressing covering the right side of his face and had lost his eye, half his face and his tongue. Dreadful, mutilating surgery, for a man who had a terminal disease anyway. He was very ill for many days, and the Sister and Staff Nurse did his dressings. I felt so sorry for him. His appearance was now awful and he was required to have Radiotherapy as well. I do not think he lasted long as the cancer had spread to other parts of his body and I felt this horrible surgery was experimental and should not have been done at all. He had to go back to his little village in rural Cornwall looking like a monster and the effect this had on his nearest and dearest was not hard to imagine.

Junior Nurses were not encouraged to express opinions about this sort of thing so I kept these thoughts to myself. We could not talk but it did not stop you thinking!

Westminster Hospital did a lot of cancer treatment, and on most Wards about 50% of the patients had the disease. Treatment was crude compared to now. There was surgery, Radiotherapy and Radium needles and very few of the drugs that we now call 'Chemo'. The Palliative care was good and the Pharmacy brewed painkillers. An elixir of opiates that we called 'Jungle Juice' and this was given liberally to cancer sufferers to alleviate their terrible pain. Later as the cancer advanced injections of Morphine were given and as this drug depresses the respiratory centre the end came quickly.

At that time there were no scans or sonar and the only diagnostic tools were by X-ray examination and exploratory surgery. Often we were told a patient had cancer but the actual diagnosis was hazy.

I learned a lot about cancer. It was new to me and shocking that I was seeing young men and women of my own age with this cruel disease. There are Four Stages with it. One and two are usually curable if it's diagnosed but Stage three involves a spread of the disease to other organs and Stage four is terminal. It was a loathsome disease and over my training I was to see a lot of it.

On the Wards we were given a radiation monitor to wear. All the medical staff had them and they checked out how much radiation we were exposed to. We were constantly taking patients to X-ray, and Deep X-ray treatments, and sometimes were sent to collect radiation needle packs so there was a risk. I never heard of anyone being over-exposed and the monitors were changed every four weeks or so.

One day on the ENT I was asked by Sister McLeod to go and help in the Outpatient Clinic. I had to assist the Consultant while he did sinus washouts. He was a very unpleasant man- overbearing and patronising and I think he gave the Sister a hard time.

Trays had to be laid up with the instruments and dressings on. The Consultant sprayed anaesthetic up the patient's nose and then stuck a huge needle like probe up, and with a sickening crunch went into the sinus which he then irrigated with a pump. The whole procedure was repulsive, and it must have been awful for the patient. The callous man doing the washout didn't turn a hair and I found the morning spent there a memorably vile experience. Fortunately I was not asked to go again.

While on my first Ward I was told to take a patient to the Operating Theatre. This was a challenge and I heard a lot of staff fainted on the first trip. Determined that this would not happen to me off I went with a porter and patient on a trolley. On arrival I was told to put on a gown, shoe covers and a mask as I would be escorting the patient into the operating room. This all went fine until the anaesthetic was given. Suddenly the room started swirling round and round. A Staff Nurse caught me just before I keeled over and sat me down and pushed my head down between my legs. Having recovered I returned to the Ward where everyone seemed to know what had happened!

After that first trip everything was fine and the fainting episode never happened again. Probably the whole thing was a stress/fear reaction. Maybe it's a good thing patients make the trip lying down.

My eight weeks placement on the ENT flew by. It was a nice ward and a good start for me. On the last day the Sister signed off work experience in the Yellow Book and told me that a report was written about my performance. It was a good report and I was happy with what was said. Already a list had gone up in the Nurses Home directing the new Nurses to their second assignment.

I was to stay at the Westminster and go onto another ward adjacent to the ENT. It was a General Surgery ward, and was not destined to be a success.

SPITEFUL WARD SISTER

I felt the ward Sister, a lady called Ball took an instant dislike to me. She was tall and thin with a long, sour face and seemed to whisper and hiss rather than talk normally. She was big on cronyism and had her favourites. I was not one of them. She really was a most unpleasant woman and my stay on her ward was a lousy experience.

Most of the patients on this ward had cancer and were having surgery. There were young teenagers with Sarcomas (bone cancers) and they were losing legs or arms, in attempts to amputate the disease. Others had bowel and stomach cancers and were also scheduled for surgery. It was not a happy place to work. Many of the patients were not going to make it, in spite of the surgery and treatments on offer. It was devastating for the families of all of them, especially the young people and harrowed parents visited daily, and frequently the priest would visit to say prayers. The Ward always seemed hushed and no laughter was heard or chatting as was usual in most other places.

I did my first Night Duty on this Ward. We began the shift at 8.45 pm and started in the Sister's office with a report. Work was allocated, lights turned down, and most of the patients were offered night sedation with the drug round. Some had observations done every half an hour so they did not get much sleep. Staff numbers were at a minimum. One Staff Nurse and two Juniors, one in the Men's Ward and one for the Women's. At 9pm we took round a trolley with milky drinks. There was tea too but we encouraged patients to have Horlicks or Ovaltine to try and get a good night's rest.

At about Midnight I was sent for a coffee break. This was held in a room in the Hospital and was a nice cup of caffeine laced coffee and a delicious sticky bun. We all sat together, but no-one spoke. There was total silence as white faced, sleep deprived girls contemplated another eight hours work.

At about 2am I would be sent to get a meal break in the Nurses Home dining room. This was accessed by a tunnel that ran from the Hospital to Queen Mary's Home. It was a nerve wracking trip that started out from the basement, ran right past the Morgue and then the long trek through the tunnel. It was twilight light, and only very seldom did you meet anyone else. I was very uneasy about this spooky journey, but if you wanted to eat there was no choice.

At 6am we would start bathing very sick patients. It was a point of pride to get as much work done as possible to save the morning staff the basics as there was always a lot to do then with Operating lists and attendant care.
We finished the shift at 7.45am, and having been on duty for 11 hours, went for breakfast prior to going to bed. Sleeping was another issue as our body clocks protested. We did a week of nights and then had a few days off. It was hard and I never got used to the disruption of having to work these hours every four weeks.

Sister Ball floated around the ward whispering to patients and directing Nurse care. She had a critical manner and no matter how hard you tried, you could never get it right for her.
She seemed to be possessive about patients, and would monopolise them somehow.
I recall one lady on the ward called Mrs Bain. She had cancer of the tongue and had experienced a partial resection (removal) in an attempt to cut out the malignancy. It had failed and the disease had spread. She was in terrible pain as you can imagine and each day I had the job of irrigating her mouth with a Higgin's syringe (rubber pump) to remove the horrible build up of pus and dead tissue. I did this as gently as I could with warmed saline, but over a few days I noticed she got weaker, and her pain more intense.
In the report Sister Ball discussed Mrs Bain, and obviously the poor woman was not one of her favourites. She said that she was not very ill, and implied that hypochondria was present. I was angry at this and spoke up, saying that Mrs Bain was in terrible pain and very ill. I added that she needed Morphine as the 'Jungle Juice 'was not touching her.
This lessee majesty earned me a withering look and reprimand. Our relationship never recovered and I rightly anticipated a bad report when I left the ward.
After two days off, on my return to the ward , I learned that Mrs Bain had died the previous day. This event was not mentioned much, but I knew it had proved my plea for her.
This whole episode left a nasty taste in my mouth and put me right off nursing and I decided to explore options to leave and find another career.

There was no going back to the Newspaper. That door was closed. Also the wages would not really support accommodation as I had been subsidised with Aunty Dot.
I heard that a large multinational company did a secretarial training and applied for this seeing it as a way out of my dilemma. I got an interview with a rather unpleasant, tweed clad woman. She told me during the interview that she was a friend of Lavinia Young the Westminster Matron and that was the end of that. Whether or not this was reported back I had no idea, but it seemed I now had a choice of going back to live with Hilda and Reg or sticking out a very hard time. After a lot of thought the Nursing won and I knew I had to stay. There was simply no option.

GRITTING ONE'S TEETH

Because of the bad report I was called to the Assistant Matrons office for a 'discussion'!
This woman was a real martinet and I expected the worst, maybe even the sack. In the event she was surprisingly nice to me and encouraged me to keep trying and said it would be much easier in the second year of training. She did not refer to the bad report and certainly another chance was being offered. Obviously if I had been booted out I would have no option but to go home. Aunty Dorothy could not be leant on again. It was not fair on her to overcrowd her home so the offer to carry on was a relief. The thought of returning to my horrible parents suddenly made the hard work and poor pay of nursing seem attractive!
After eight weeks with nasty Sister Ball a transfer was made to a new Hospital and placement .This was All Saints Hospital in Lambeth on the gynaecological ward with a Sister Knox. The

ward was obviously all women and I had to travel by bus to get to work. On top of that fares had to be paid and this all came out of the measly salary. You would think the Hospital would pay the fares but no! It was my money that went although as I travelled in uniform with my red lined nurse's cloak and straw bonnet, the bus conductor sometimes gave me a free ride. All Saints was a really old building, unlike the Westminster which was fairly new. The ward seemed to twist and turn with nooks and crannies everywhere. Sister Knox appeared nice but aloof and it was difficult to get a take on her.

I soon settled in and was told that the work shift included a stretch of night duty. Again I found this very testing. The hospital worked a swizzle on our hours with the night shift. It ran from 8.45pm to 8 am. However we were given two hours off in the night which we could not take for geographical reasons, but this usefully depressed the hours worked.

I had about an hour break in total so over the eight nights worked the hospital got free hours. Although we worked long hours, weekends and Bank Holidays there was no overtime payments or extras. This was how it was and no arguments.

It was winter whist working in Lambeth and it was cold at night. The patients stayed tucked up in bed but at 3 am one felt cold and exhausted. Sleeping was not easy in the Nurses Home with banging doors and shouting voices, but when you are really tired you do get off and sleep deep.

We worked a rota of nights and mixed earlies and 1 to 9's. As usual I did lots of swaps and managed plenty of luxury lie-ins and rests.

There was a Library in Great Smith Street just a short walk from the Nurses Home and I enjoyed loads of books and visited as often as possible. This was free and a great help to the financially challenged like myself.

I couldn't help but notice that there were a lot of dirty scruffy men in the Library mostly reading the papers. I later learned that there was a Salvation Army hostel near bye and a refuge for down and outs and tramps .The Library was warm with comfy seats so many spent the day here. Quite a few turned up at the Westminster hoping for a free bed for the night. They were not very attractive as they were filthy dirty and frequently verminous. Sometimes they really had a health issue but mostly they fabricated symptoms just to get Board and lodging on the NHS!

My stay on the ward at All Saints was prior to the Abortion Act. In spite of that I saw a lot of both natural and un-natural miscarriages. It was really very upsetting to see what were termed 'the products of conception' in a pool of blood in a bedpan. Beautiful, little babies of just three months gestation. Tiny hands and feet and closed sleeping eyes. It was so sad and their mums were frequently devastated and in floods of tears. Sometimes I would find five or six bedpans in the sluice each with its tiny deceased baby. It broke my heart and you wondered how nature could be so cruel?

I had my nineteenth birthday in October and with my friends Chris and Bau celebrated with cake and lemonade. There was nothing from Hilda and Reg ,not even a card. My friends asked what I got for my birthday and I lied rather than admit I had nothing. They both gave me gifts. I knew my sisters Margaret and Maxine had no money even to send a card and I did not hear from Susan either. My Aunts had not sent anything since pre-Aden times so I had rather a lean time.

I did have a bit of really good luck at this time. Prior to Nursing I bought myself a pair of mushroom coloured, suede shoes. I never liked them but decided to wear them as I really could not afford to waste anything. On the first wearing the sole tore away from the upper. Normally I would have just thrown them away. Being skint I decided to take then back to the

shop where I had bought them, which was part of a major chain of shoe shops. Duly returned the shop promised to try and repair them. I was asked to call in the following week and when I did learned that the shoes were un-repairable and a voucher for the full amount was to be given. These were sale shoes so it was very generous of the shop. I was desperately short of black stockings and asked if it was possible to get these with the voucher instead of another pair of shoes. The shop said this was fine and so I became the proud owner of fifteen pairs of black stockings. To say I was delighted was an understatement. This was potentially a whole years supply when usually I struggled to buy a single pair.
It must have been the best deal I ever made.

MAKING MISTAKES WITH 'FRIENDS'

At this time I made friends with a very religious girl called Lizl. She was a 'Born Again' Christian and had obviously decided to convert me to her extremist beliefs. I had a battering from her in subtle ways and she wanted me to go to the Nurses Christian Union meetings. Because she was so pushy I refused to go which with hindsight was a stupid mistake. I would have made friends and re-connected with my Christian faith. It would have given me a spiritual understanding for my work, and manageable social life and later I regretted this decision.
Lizl took me to see Billy Graham at Wembley and was upset when I did not respond to his call to "Go Forward". Billy and his performance did not impress at all, but Lizl did not give up and persisted in her friendship which I realised later was merely a ruse to effect the conversion she wanted. She was very artistic and found the Nursing very difficult to cope with and was talking about leaving.
One weekend she invited me to her home to meet her family. They lived in Enfield and her dad was a University Professor and she had three sisters and a nice mum. That same weekend Jennifer invited me out and I cancelled this to go with Lizl. Jennifer got really angry at this and said that if I did not join her it was the end of our friendship and she would never speak to me again. This ultimatum angered me so I ignored the threat and joined Lizl. Jennifer kept her word and I never saw her again which was sad after two years of friendship.
Lizl's family were all very religious and one of the daughters was a rebel and struck out against the prayerful and narrow family. She became pregnant at 16 and was sent to a Mother and baby home and the child was put up for adoption. The Lizl family rose to this challenge by dismissing Laura and her pregnancy, and only accepted her back in the family with the baby removed. It must have been hard on Laura and Lizl was shocked and full of prayers and admonishment for Laura.
I wondered if the parents ever regretted the loss of their first grandchild?

Lizl told me she had once seen a ghost. I was surprised she admitted this as it was not really in keeping with her belief system. She had been to a Lake in the country somewhere and with her artist materials sat painting the scene. Whilst doing this she saw a lady by the Lake dressed in a long dress of a bygone age fashion. She stared at this apparition and then it suddenly faded and disappeared. I was interested in the paranormal and knew that she was telling the truth.

Whilst staying with Lizl we visited gardens that were owned by her dad's employer, London University and were full of experimental and medicinal plants. When I got home both my legs had massive bleeding under the skin and were terribly and extensively bruised. Obviously one of the plants had caused a severe allergy and the cause was never identified. In spite of my problem I went to work and with the black Nursing stockings I wore no one really noticed the horrible mess I was in.

Lizl finally left Nursing after six months. She said she could not stand the suffering and pain of the patients and she planned to go to Art School. Before she left she sold me a Nurses Text book of Anatomy and Physiology, and wrote in it -"Annette paid me 30 shillings for this book and did not steal it! Ha ha". Obviously she had a very low regard for my morality and after she went I never heard nor saw her again.

I continued to live in the Nurses home that was sans everything. No electrics in my room and no facility for making tea or coffee. If you wanted a drink it was water or squash that you purchased yourself.
My main enjoyment was a gustatory one and as soon as my monthly cheque came in I would withdraw £2 and set off for a supermarket in Victoria. This was a clandestine experience as I had to creep around to avoid the manager spotting me. He was a South African and if he saw me he would rush out of his office and chat me up. I think he had a two way mirror!
He would follow me all round the supermarket asking me out and seemed totally obsessed. I always told him I was too busy and tired to go out with him but he was very persistent and a nuisance. The supermarket was cheap and the squash, chocolate and peanuts were just what I wanted but I dreaded this man's attentions and would bulk buy to reduce visits to the minimum.
Chris and Bau would come with me shopping sometimes , and found this ardent suitor to be highly amusing ,and teased me about him. He must have been at least 30 years and much too old for me.
Chris and Bau were now my only friends. After six months in Nursing I had lost touch with everyone else and relied on them for support and camaraderie .
Bau came from Singapore but had been educated in the UK at a Christian boarding school. She was friendly and fun. Always giggling and laughing and was an excellent Student Nurse, getting good reports and finding favour with the Ward Sisters. Her family were very wealthy and owned a chain of Hotels in the Far East. Bau , unlike me wanted for nothing but in spite of her privileged background she was down to earth ,friendly and cheerful.
Chris was from the Irish Republic and a real Colleen, with black hair, a very fair skin and green eyes. Again she had good family support and had been to a 'Finishing School' in London prior to her starting Nursing and had done modelling and deportment and a Cordon Bleu cookery course. Part of this training involved working in a top London food outlet, where she seemed to spend her time eating smoked salmon and other delicacies. She had lots of interesting stories to tell of this experience, and also wrote Articles for Upmarket magazines and earned a lot of money from them. Both my friends were cheerful and in the same boat of long hours, and little free time. We would go to the cinema together and spend ages talking, discussing our patients, experiences and duties. The friendships were the mainstay of my existence.

Christmas was approaching and time had flown by. I was relaxed on the Ward and had learned many skills. All the PTS training was put to good use and other things were taught on the Ward. The work Rotas were up and I saw I was working Christmas but had the New Year off. Everyone told me that Christmas on the Ward was a wonderful experience and I would have a great time. Most of the patients would be sent home and apart from emergencies our duties would be light. This information did not impress much as my idea of Christmas was a nice, big, turkey dinner and putting my feet up! Still there was no choice and no argument and I resigned myself to the inevitable .

About a week before Christmas the Ward Sister announced that there would be a Party for all the Nurses and I saw that I was free to attend this. There was to be a turkey dinner and various extra treats of chocolates and other goodies donated by patients and reserved for this Christmas blow out.
The meal was a very formal function. We all had to be in full uniform, with our red lined cloaks, and Sister Knox sat at the head of the table. One of the donations on offer was Asti Spumante wine as a case had been given by a grateful patient. A lot of the Nurses declined this alcoholic wine, but finding it delicious, I got stuck in and consumed several glasses. I got a bit tipsy and started talking loudly and cracking jokes. This broke the somewhat frosty atmosphere of the gathering and Sister Knox seemed to appreciate this as soon everyone was chattering and giggling and the party was a big success. I won the approval of Sister Knox that night and got a good report when I left all due to my performance at this party.

On the Ward one day I got asked to go and supervise a doctor's examination of a young woman. I was to be the Chaperone and ensure that everything was done in a proper manner. The woman aged about 22 was French and her diagnosis was Dyspareunia (painful sexual intercourse). There was a really sleazy atmosphere round this woman and I learned she was a high class prostitute and probably her condition was work related. She did have a sensational figure, and obviously had a big impact on men. She behaved like she had some terrible affliction, groaning, gasping, clutching her stomach and sighing. I felt annoyed that she was given so much attention for a rather trivial complaint. The doctors absolutely fawned on her! No doubt after discharge she put her charges up and bonked less to reduce her symptoms.

Another patient on this ward was a very sad case. A spinster lady with terminal, Ovarian cancer. She was in the last stages of this disease and was to spend the rest of her limited time in hospital, as she had no family to care for her. She was a nice lady with a sweet, quiet demeanour. She was not demanding and tended to get sidelined for other more vocal patients. One day during the report Sister Knox got into a huge temper and said this lady was not being properly cared for and had been found to have a nasty dose of headlice which needed urgent treatment. We had no idea how she had caught them, but she had long, thick hair and getting rid of the lice was a challenge to say the least. About a week after the headlice treatment this poor woman passed away. We all missed her. She was like a fixture in the Ward and her passing left a gap. I would look at her bed space and feel sad. She was a lovely, dignified lady who sat and waited patiently for her days to end.

At the New Year I was to leave All Saints after three months and go back to the Wolfson Nursing School for more training. The short days and weekends off were a welcome break but I had enjoyed my time at All Saints and wondered where my next placement would be after the school?

BACK TO THE NURSE'S SCHOOL

The school was now upgrading our abilities. One thing we now had to learn was giving an injection ; both intra- muscular and sub-dermal. We were shown how to 'draw up' the injectable substance, excluding air (this could cause an air embolus if injected and potentially kill the patient) and how and where to stick the needle into flesh. After plunging the needle in you had to draw the plunger back to ensure you had not hit a vein. Any blood, and you had to do it again. In hundreds of injections given I never saw blood! The other thing learned was that you gave the injection in the left, upper, outer quadrant of the buttock area to avoid hitting the sciatic nerve. I was always worried about this. We were not taught how to give an arm jab, and I never really felt confident with the procedure.

Our Nursing school left a lot of stuff out that we needed to know, but we were not aware of this as were constantly told how lucky we were to have the attendance opportunity. It was only when I took my written finals that I realised how much had not been covered.

We practiced the injections on oranges as these have the resistance of human tissue. It seemed easy with the oranges but transferring this to living flesh was another matter.

In those days Nurses were not allowed to initiate Intra-Venous drips. We were instead taught how to prepare the IV trolley for the Doctor with 'Giving Sets' and dressings and a splint to secure the patients arm. I recall one Nurse I worked with really annoyed me with her wasteful approach to the IV. She would lay up a trolley with two types of Giving Sets on it for the doctor to choose his preference. Fine- but she would then open up both of them so they were no longer sterile and one of them had to be thrown away. She was senior to me so I could not say anything but raged at this waste of Health Service funds as these sets were very expensive.

A lot of waste went on and the Nurses were often extravagant with bed linen and clinical items. I saw nurses use handfuls of incontinence pads when one would have done. Everything was thrown away and no one it seemed counted the cost.

Other things learned in school were 'The Last Offices'. What to do with a dead patient and how to prepare the body for the mortuary. This was a bit grim but was necessary. The body was to be washed and the hair combed. The eyes were closed and a hospital, white, paper shroud was put on. There was a label with the deceased's name and hospital number and this was tied to the patient's big toe. We were told that there should always be two Nurses present for this last act of respect for the patient, and prayers should be said, and thought and respect given for the religion of the deceased. In some cases if a Jewish person passed we were not to lay out the body but call the family as special rituals had to be performed by the Rabbi, and I think the same applied to Islamics.

Every day in the school we were taught new procedures like giving drugs with two Nurses checking and the Law regarding the DDA's.

These dangerous and addictive drugs were counted as to misuse them was a criminal act. Two Nurses had to check out the Morphine or other listed drug, observe it being drawn up into a syringe, sign the DDA Book, and then both go to the patient to observe its proper administration. This was taken very seriously by the Nursing hierarchy and it was rammed home how important it was to observe the protocols.

We were taught how to bandage post-operative wounds and how to do a 'stump dressing' on an amputated limb. This was quite a skill to do as it had to stay on and be firm enough to help the healing wound stay in shape. I enjoyed doing these and could do one to a high standard. I had plenty of practice later with amputees on the Orthopaedic ward and took great pride in a good result.

We were told that a lot of patients were allergic to the standard zinc oxide plaster, and special non-allergenic plaster called Micropore was to be used. This was expensive and should have been administered frugally but many of the Nurses were extravagant with it and again wasted money and resources, pulling out yards of the stuff when a tiny piece was needed

There was a lesson on taking out stitches after surgery and the specific way to cleanse wounds so as to avoid infection. There was a non-touch (aseptic) technique taught where forceps and not fingers were deployed. There were latex, surgical gloves available but these were seldom given out as they were very expensive. I only ever saw them used on the ward for rectal examinations and in the operating theatre. Nurses were expected to wash their hands before and after doing a dressing and in fact any patient centred procedure to try and avoid cross infections .I always remembered the Agar plates from the Tropical Medicine Hospital and was very conscientious about hand washing.

We had lectures from a variety of Doctors on many subjects and also were shown films about medical conditions. It was pretty awful seeing these films and they should have been X rated! Two in particular stand out.

One was about the condition known as Aortic aneurism. This is where the main artery to the body (the Aorta) develops a weakness in the wall and balloons out. With the pressure of the heart pumping it can burst and is catastrophic, causing instant death. In the film this was all explained plus a really horrible, gory scene of the mortuary and the Pathologist plunging his hands into a bloody body cavity. It was a repulsive sight and none of the Nurses were happy watching it.

Nowadays with heart by-pass machinery abdominal aneurism can be repaired, but this was not available in the 1960's and sufferers just died sudden deaths.

There was also a film about eye surgery and this showed an eye being enucleated (removed) in full and graphic detail. A lot of the students watching this started screaming and my friend Bau nearly fainted as she was phobic about eyes anyway.

It was all memorably unpleasant but we Nurses were expected to cope with any shocking sight or sound and no consideration was given to the fact that we were still rather naive teenagers.

At the latter end of the School fortnight we were all taken on a visit to the Westminster Children's Hospital to have a look round and see the type of work done there.

The Hospital was not very old and it was strange to see the tiny cots and cradles instead of the big hospital beds I was used to. Most of the sick children lay quietly and I noticed how kind and caring all the staff were. We had Children's Nurse students join us in the School sometimes. They were girls who loved children and there was a very high drop-out rate when they realised that with sick kids it was not all cuddles and fun. Someone had to hold these tots down when painful procedures were performed, and that someone was the Children's Nurse!

We saw the surgical patients and the medical. One horrible thing was a Ward of babies in cots who were not expected to live longer than a few days. Two had Anencephaly-a form of congenital monstrosity. They were born with hardly any brain and their condition was not compatible with survival. It was painful to see these little mites who had no hope, and at the end of the trip I was glad to be doing General Nursing. I felt it took a very special person to care for these beautiful children, and manage the sad happenings that were an inevitable fact. The Children's Nurses seemed to tick the box!

The work was intensive and we were schooled to go onto the Wards and cope with anything thrown at us.

So much information was given in the school and we were now ten months into our training. No longer raw recruits but experienced with all manner of disease and suffering and finding increased confidence as our learning gained momentum. We were being prepared to take responsibility for vulnerable sick people and it was important that we got it right.

School time flew and the List appeared with our new Ward destinations. I saw I was to go to the Children's Ward, and was somewhat apprehensive about this. I was not a very patient person and realised caring for sick kids would be difficult.

I remained living in the grotty Nurses home but found out if I was away overnight I could sign the absence book and get a rebate on my board and lodging charges. This could enhance the salary as much as £5 over a month and was a very welcome discovery.

Another thing was that Susan's mother in law a Doris Perkins had heard that I was in London and invited me for lunch one Sunday. Doris was twice married but now a self-supporting widow and was Caretaker/Secretary to several doctors in a Harley Street practice. With the job she got a salary and free Basement flat where she lived with Alex's half brother and sister. I was pleased with the invitation and clutching a small box of chocolates turned up for the meal and meeting.
I immediately liked Doris. She was bright, humorous and a really kind and caring person. She asked about my Nursing and I unloaded my problems. She was sympathetic and was appalled when she heard about my accommodation and insisted on giving me a saucepan to make soup. Doris had been at Susan's wedding but we had not been introduced. I was so pleased to meet this chatty, urbane woman and felt Susan was lucky to have such a mother in law.

We had a splendid lunch and Susan was present. She was working as a Temp Secretary in London and coining it in. It soon became apparent that Doris did not like Susan much and no doubt saw through her veneer of pleasantry to the spiteful young woman who had ensnared her son. Susan was pregnant already and due fairly soon. It was a 'Honeymoon baby' and she now lived with Alex in Oakham in Rutland. Alex was away on exercises with his Squadron so Susan pitched up in London to fill her pockets.
Doris told me to visit anytime I liked. We really clicked and it was the first non- nursing friend I had found since I started the training.

CHALLENGING KIDS!

The Children's ward was worse than I imagined. It was not general health conditions but almost exclusively Heart problems either needing dangerous surgery or terminal care. For me it was a disaster.
For a start I did not feel comfortable with toddlers and kids. I had always regarded my younger sisters as a liability and had been full- time nurse maid to them for many years. Now I was supposed to transform into a cuddly, mumsy Nurse who had loads of empathy with babies and young children.
The Ward Sister was a bit non-descript and seemed easy to please but there was a Staff Nurse who seemed to be on my every shift and she was downright unpleasant. Nothing I did was right! She would screech and shout at me going red in the face and shaking.
The children on the Ward were difficult for a variety of reasons. Many had chronic conditions that could not be treated until the heart had grown to an operable size and they were used to hospital and knew the ropes better than I did. Most of them were demanding and spoilt and it seemed that every whim must be indulged.
There would be demands for ice-cream or biscuits. "I want" was the order of the day and the nasty Staff Nurse decided that when these kids said "Jump" I wasn't going high enough.
A Night duty occasion was a total disaster.
One of the badly behaved kids aged about 12 had surgery for a heart defect and was under special surveillance in a private room. He had an IV and this had to be checked along with his

pulse and blood pressure. I did his observations and then went onto other duties. The next thing was the Staff Nurse screaming at me that the IV had run through. This was bad and I felt responsible. She put up another IV and told me to watch it carefully. After 10 minutes of staying in the kids room and seeing the drip running slowly I left and went to do other duties of which there were many. Ten minutes later another shriek rang out. The IV had run out again and it was all my fault. The abuse went on and on and I felt terrible. I'm pretty sure the wretched kid had turned the IV on full as soon as I left the room. There was no other explanation , but according to the Staff Nurse it was entirely my fault and confirmed my utter incompetence in her eyes.
She ranted about this for the rest of the shift and made a huge deal out of the problem with the Ward Sister. I could see another bad report looming and was glad to get off duty.
Later I was to see this Staff Nurse losing her temper with a child of about 8 years who cheeked her. She physically picked him up and forcefully threw him on the bed shouting at him. This was abuse and well out of order but I said nothing and she got away with it.
The worst thing about this Ward was with the terminal neonates that came in. These babies had inoperable heart conditions and were destined to die. Fallot's tetralogy, Coarction of the Aorta and Transposition of the main vessels were all beyond the surgery of the day. Once heart by-pass machines were invented surgical correction could be done, but in the Sixties there was no remedy.
These full- term, beautiful babies did not feed and lay gasping for every breath. Parents were told not to visit and over two or three days they became weaker and then passed. Watching them was truly horrible and it was so upsetting that functionality became difficult. Observing these little mites you became frozen to the spot. There was nothing to be done and you just had to accept the inevitable. I really did not enjoy this Ward at all.
 Mornings were a nightmare. I never had a baby to bath but always a difficult, wriggling, squirming un-cooperative toddler who would yell loudly at the sight of a wash cloth. I usually ended up more wet and bothered than the kid. It was all frustrating and made me feel totally inadequate.
We had some long stay patients on the Ward and one was a tiny little girl called Sharon. She weighed only 9 pounds and was 10 months old. She had a gross inoperable heart defect but somehow had fought and survived. We all liked to give her a feed and a cuddle. Each suck of the bottle was an effort for her and she would gasp and turn blue with each mouthful. In spite of this we could get milk down her if time and patience were given. I think she should have been spooned solids and had a spouted cup, as the effort of sucking from the bottle was too much for her. I was not experienced enough to suggest this and no one else mooted the idea.

After eight gruelling weeks I went to the Sisters office for my report. I was expecting the worst but in fact it wasn't too bad. The Sister confirmed what I knew and that was that Children's Nursing was not for me but she said I had tried hard and mostly worked to an acceptable standard. The nasty Staff Nurse was present during this interview and glared at me. I was only glad it was not she that was writing the report or I think the result would have been summary dismissal!

The Swinging Sixties were happening outside the Hospital Wards and most people of my age were having a great time. Pop music, The Beatles and Rolling Stones, Carnaby Street and Biba. Fashion clothing and lots of fun.
All this passed me by. I was totally out of touch with reality and compressed into the medical world and the burden of Nursing. What you don't know you don't miss and so I plodded on as the total lack of cash cut most things out anyway.

One perk Nurses did get was free Theatre tickets. When a show was not full spare tickets would be given to the Nurses' Homes, and frequently these were available. Some of the productions were really good and we would get the best seats. I saw 'the Mousetrap' which was excellent and many other things. It was a free night out and this was just as well as I could not even afford a drink in the interval.

The best thing I saw was at the Royal Opera House. One grateful patient had left all the Nurses on the ward a note of introduction to his Theatre agent. We could have two seats for any production we liked and I chose to see 'A Midsummer Night's Dream' ballet. It was wonderful, a truly transporting experience. Chris came with me and enjoyed it too.

I wrote to the patient and thanked him for his kind gift and told him how much the trip had been enjoyed. He replied that he was pleased that Chris and I had such a good time but out of all the Nurses on the Ward I was the only one to have taken up his offer.

The other thing the Nurses got was a lot of chocolates. Many kind patients left boxes for the Nursing staff on their departure and every day there were open boxes to tuck into. This did not help my weight at all, and on top of that patients would have sweets and other goodies and were more than happy to share them.

Susan had her baby at the end of January in 1967, a little boy called Alex junior. I was invited to visit to see him and on five nights off travelled to Oakham by train to see this new nephew. He was a cute baby and it was hard to believe that this sister was now a mother and responsible for this tiny sprot. She was bottle feeding and seemed to take about an hour to perform the feed. I said I would do it as with my heart babies had experience of slow feeders and knew every trick of the trade to hurry things up. However it was no good. Alex was a sleepy baby and would not suck. He would take a mouthful of milk and then go to sleep. I tried hard to wake him but it took me an hour to get three ounces of milk down him as well. He was worse than baby Sharon and that was saying something.

Susan exhibited incredible patience with him and feeding three hourly became a full-time job. Susan had reverted to her slutty, unwashed state. Her hair was a greasy mess and face festooned with blackheads. I don't think washing and personal hygiene were high on the agenda either. She seemed to have no idea about presenting herself in an attractive fashion and had few feminine traits. She was quite pretty but never bothered to adorn herself or enhance her appearance. She had just let herself go.

Also she was totally obsessed with money and talked non-stop about Alex's big salary and how she intended to work when her infant was older. On and on she went about money and the material acquisitions she aspired to. It was sad. There was no money in Nursing but such greed was unacceptable even to the financially deprived like me.

I don't know what Alex thought about his wife's appearance but the marriage foundered some years later and I'm sure her sluttiness and money-grubbing were contributory factors. She never managed to look smart or well groomed. Once Hilda was off the scene Susan reverted to type and looked awful.

The other thing that amused me was that while in Cyprus Susan and I had jointly purchased a record player. I wanted to pay her out and take ownership as it was usable in the UK. Susan refused and with Hilda's support paid me out, and kept the player for herself.

It was in her house and while there decided to play a record. I switched the machine on and lifted the playing arm to the record. I got a really bad electric shock and obviously the player was not earthed or something and so was useless! It served her right. She had lost her money and I was fortunate not to have this useless item. Alex had all the equipment she needed and she could have let me keep it for my Nursing.

CASUALTY

On my return to the Hospital my new placement was on Casualty. I was a bit scared about this and wondered what horrible sights I would be exposed to. In this respect I was lucky and the biggest' yuk' moment was seeing an in-growing toenail removed.
Every day on duty I was in the Admissions area and a constant flow of ambulant (walking) patients turned up with a whole variety of problems that the medics and Nurses were supposed to sort. There were cuts, broken limbs, burns and serious illnesses; along with hypochondriacs, tramps and freeloaders. I spent a lot of the day putting on dressings and bandaging wounds. I worked to instruction and it was a bit nerve wracking as you never knew what would be thrown at you next. The Doctor would treat a patient-Stitch a wound, cut out a foreign body or whatever and leave me to dress the wound and discharge the patient. It was a busy production line and I found myself working non-stop.
We gave a lot of Tetanus shots for people with dirty wounds or animal bites. I must have given dozens .One day a young man came in with a large Ampoule with Procaine Penicillin in it. He required that this be given and out of my sight the substance was drawn up into a large syringe.
The Duty Staff Nurse called me over and said I was to give it.
The patient was in a cubicle and I got him to lie on his side so I could inject his buttock. I plunged the needle in and drew back as best I could. No blood so I proceeded- or at least tried to. The thick substance would not inject. I kept up a downward force and very, very slowly the white mixture went in. It took me over ten minutes to get the 50 ml injection completed. When finished I apologised to the patient for the pain I must have caused him, but he was very nice about it and said it didn't hurt and I'd done a good job.
Later the Staff Nurse told me he was a Homosexual rent boy and had Syphilis. She set me up with the injection as no warning was given. Senior staff found this sort of thing highly amusing but to me it was a nightmare.
This young man was lucky to have a cure for his disease as at that time the Wards had many dementia patients suffering from GPI (General Paralysis of the Insane) which is Terminal Syphilis. Many were old soldiers from the First World War and had returned from France with this then untreatable disease and had entered a vegetative state in old age as the brain was affected and damaged.

There was a big burns clinic held once a week in Casualty and the afflicted would be booked in to have their wound checked by a doctor, cleansed and bound up.
One day I was assigned to run this Clinic and felt a bit overwhelmed by the responsibility. The Waiting Room was full of patients and using their Files I Started to call them in one at a time.
I would remove the dirty dressing and expose the wound and then seek out the Doc to come and check things out. Once this was done using aseptic technique, I would redress the wound and discharge the patient, having given out a new appointment. This went well for several patients and then I called in a Mr Wright. I looked at his notes and it said that he had a thigh burn. Without consulting him and in a hurry I told him to take his trousers off and get on the examination table. He looked a bit surprised but did what he was told. I ran off to get the Doc in and then hurried back to remove the dressing. I looked at his thigh but could see nothing." Where is your dressing?" I asked. Mr Wright waved his hand which had a big bandage on it.

No wonder he had looked at me oddly when asked to take his trousers off. I felt most embarrassed and told him to get his trousers back on pronto. By the time the Doc arrived he was sitting in a chair, trousers back on, with his hand burn on display and no one but me and the patient aware of my mistake. In fact there were two Mr Wrights that morning and I had the wrong one in.

Even in 1967 there was a shortage of Nursing and Medical Staff and we were seeing more and more foreigners working in the NHS. I was assigned to night duty on Casualty and was as usual ushering the queue of patients to see the Doc.
One was an Arab looking family with the woman in a Burka.
I didn't think anything of this and sent her in to see the medic. Suddenly - about five minutes later I heard an enraged shout from the curtained cubicle. The South African Doc on duty emerged from the curtains shouting "Get the hell out of here"
The Egyptians - for that was their nationality, ran for the exit chased by the red faced and angry Doc.
Once they had disappeared he calmed down and explained that the woman had presented with a chronic, long-term fungal disease which the Doc had seen before. She should have had treatment for this in her own country, but instead had taken a flight to the UK for free treatment which was apparently the cheaper option.
She was an Egyptian national and as a non- emergency was not entitled to treatment.
I was a bit shocked at the violence of the reaction here but realised that someone at least was protecting the NHS resources. I am sure if it had been a British Doc the woman would have been admitted to the hospital and given free and very expensive treatment.
It was highly likely that the Egyptians would visit another hospital and try their luck again. A lot of this abuse continues with 'Health Tourists' visiting the UK for free healthcare. The system urgently needs tightening up but little or nothing is done to prevent it. It was down to a South African to protect us from this exploitation and he certainly did a good job on this occasion.

My eight weeks on Casualty passed quickly. I never saw any bad road traffic accidents and the worst patients were filthy, drunk men who were sleeping rough and came to us hoping for a free bed for the night. Most had head lice and other vermin. Sometimes we bathed them, and I think the Hospital had an arrangement with the Salvation Army Hostel near bye and they would be sent there.
I heard that there was a swimming pool in Great Smith Street but decided not to go in spite of my love for swimming as these dirty men were rumoured to go for a swim to clean themselves up. After what I had seen in Casualty could not stomach the thought of sharing the water.

I remained living in the Queen Mary Nurses home and Chris and Bau were my room- mates. If we had mutual free time we would go out shopping or to the Cinema but this depended on my funds which were often low or non-existent.
Chris was very intelligent but was a depressive personality. Sometimes she would be cheerful and sociable and other times would close her door and refuse to answer callers.
We had a maid who cleaned our rooms once a week and we also had a clean sheet and would sort our beds out to keep them fresh. Sometimes Chris would not let her in and the Maid would come tapping on my door asking for help. There was nothing to be done. Chris refused to respond to pleas and requests and her door remained closed to the world. I think Chris really suffered with this 'Black Dog' hounding her. She would say strange things. One being that she half believed she was the only person alive and that her life was some sort of sick

joke. One time when we were crossing Vauxhall Bridge Road to go to the Cinema we nearly got run over. Just prior to this incident she had been talking about there being no point in living etc. I had agreed with her but then pointed out that for two potential suicides we had been mighty careful with ourselves crossing the dangerous road! This had her in fits of laughter and she cheered up. I found that if I could make a joke in her despair she could cope and would lighten up. Really I was very worried about her.

At about this time I learned of an employment Agency in London and realised I could get paid work babysitting and doing light cooking on my days off.
Chris decided to do this too, mostly for gaining material for her writings and articles. Bau declined. She did not need the cash and would sit laughing when we told her of our exploits. I certainly met some very odd people on the Agency bookings.
The first booking was to babysit a small girl whilst the parents went out for the evening. She was very sweet and no trouble at all. I had to be back at the Nurses Home by 11.30pm or was locked out for the night and would be in trouble if I was not in by then.
The couple got back at 11pm and paid me £1.50 which was good money and also refunded my fares and paid a taxi to take me home.
The taxi driver took me to the wrong destination. Well out of the way and I began to panic and could see the Nurse's Home doors closing. The stupid man redirected himself and with a lot of urging from me arrived at 11.29pm, so I just made it. This put me off the babysitting for a bit, but the nice couple rang again and I was free the night they wanted.
Again all went well except that when they got home there had obviously been a row. It appeared that the man was a film director and they had been to the Premiere performance of a Musical he had directed. He seemed to be really down on his wife who was a lovely lady and tried to involve me in the row as he made spiteful criticisms of her and it was all most embarrassing. I did not agree with what he was saying and just wanted to get home.
He finally called me a taxi and I cleared off; he really was very nasty to his wife which was unfair and offensive. They did not ask for me again so maybe they realised that he at least had gone too far.

I had five days off after a week of nights on Casualty and got asked to go and do some Day babysitting for a family in St John's Wood.
By the name I realised they were Jewish and wondered what to expect. I had experience of Orthodox Jews in the hospital and knew that there might be various restrictions.
Firstly I was asked to mind the two kids which was what I was contracted to do. Then could I just put the Hoover round? Next the whole house needed dusting. Also would I go and make a Cottage pie for tea? Mrs Goldberg kept up a list of demands that were nothing to do with childcare and I began to get annoyed. Whilst I was doing all this work my employer sat playing 'super mum' and read to the children.
I had six out of my eight hours doing housework. I knew this Housekeeping service cost more than the babysitting so she got me on the cheap. Needless to say although the family were obviously rolling in money she argued about my fee. She did not want to pay fares even though this was an Agency rule. I did get the money in the end from this cheapskate and her parting shot was she hoped I would come again.
She rang me two days later asking me to return to work for her. I declined and should have reported her to the Agency. However, decided against this in case I got banned from working. The money I was getting was very helpful and when I stayed over with Childcare got to claim back board and lodging from the hospital which boosted finances even further

Being based in Westminster we were close to the House of Commons. At the time Harold Wilson's Labour Party were in Government and sometimes when I came home via Westminster Tube Station I would see Mary Wilson walking her pet poodle. Security was pretty lax and she walked alone along Millbank and seemed quite relaxed and happy.
There was an MP called George Brown and he was reputed to have a drink problem. He had a high position in the Cabinet, but was unable to control his alcohol intake.
One afternoon on my way back to the Hospital, I saw him outside the gates of Parliament completely inebriated. He was holding onto the railings and fell onto the ground looking very confused and agitated. There was no one else around but it would have made a good front page story for any newspaper. George was lucky that the only witness was me and not a Tabloid reporter.
One day just as I walked past Westminster Abbey wearing my long Nurse's cloak and straw bonnet a man approached me. In stuttering English he asked "Are you Salvation Army?"
I had to laugh at this and assured him I was a Nurse and not what he thought!

Chris got herself involved with the Hospital Magazine called 'Broadway'. This glossy was run by medical students but they wanted some input from the Nurses and with her literary experience Chris was the ideal person.
She asked me to write something as well, and I did a piece on how nice it would be to have a Whippy ice cream machine in my room. Unfortunately it was obvious that whoever published it could not read my writing and the punch line which was supposed to be funny came out as meaningless drivel.
Chris wrote a piece on the hospital and medical students. I collaborated with her and it was highly abusive, making insulting remarks about both the hospital and the students.
Surprisingly it was published, and caused a lot of offence in the medical school. I think one description had been 'constipated pigeons' and this was considered highly Freudian and rude. Needless to say we were not invited to submit again.
There was not a good relationship between the Student Nurses and Doctors. Their arrogant, demanding attitude was resented.
The medical students were not a lot better and there was underlying hostility in all interactions.
A lot of medical students saw Nurses as a bedding opportunity and stories circulated about how Nurses had been used sexually and then tossed aside heartbroken. As far as possible anyone with any sense would keep well away and save themselves a whole load of trouble.

It was time to leave Casualty and again I was to remain in the Westminster and go to the General Medical Ward.
The Ward Sister on this Ward was reputed to be the kindest and nicest in the Hospital and was called Angie.
I felt I had fallen on my feet this time and was looking forward to it all.

THE NURSING EXPERIENCE GETS BETTER

Again at least 50% of the patients on this Ward had cancer. There were some really sad cases. Lovely people whom you knew would pass with this terrible disease.

Angie the Ward Sister lived up to her reputation and was really pleasant. She seemed to treat all her student Nurses with kindness and respect. She realised we needed help and there was no comparison with ghastly Sister Ball.

We would arrive on duty and gather in Angie's office where the report book was read out. Various jobs would be allocated according to Staff seniority and experience. I was no longer the most junior, and would be given more interesting tasks. Dressings, enemas and suppositories and things like injectable pain killers. We used to do pressure areas four hourly on patients. Even on the ambulant which was ridiculous. On top of that there were creature comforts to deliver, such as egg- noggs for the emaciated, and Complan protein drink for those who could not tolerate a solid diet. Some patients were tube fed and this was another task. We were sent brandy and sherry from the pharmacy as well for patients with poor appetites. It was very helpful to some of the really sick, but I heard later that the facility had been abused and was stopped.

One of my first patients was a very old spinster lady. She was a regular to the ward and demanding with it. She had severe arthritis and was in for TLC (tender loving care)
First it was extra pillows and then a hot water bottle. She wanted Complan four hourly and would make a big fuss if it didn't appear. I soon got fed up with her as it was busy so decided to do a nasty thing. I began to get her all she requested including glasses of Complan every two hours. I was most punctilious with the deliveries and the Lady was severely pressed to drink it all. I found it amusing and thought the Complan bombardment would teach her a lesson. This went on for a week throughout my shift.

At the end of the week I heard she was to be discharged. On her last afternoon she called me over. She had tears in her eyes and I wondered what she was going to say?

"Nurse Brown, my stay this time has been wonderful and it's all down to your high standards and sheer, loving kindness. Thank you so much my dear, I will never forget you".

This was not taken as a compliment but an admonishment. I realised how nasty I had been but this fragile little lady had taken me at face value. I learned a lesson right then and that was not to be a heel, and offer sincerity and good to all patients no matter how irritating they were. I thought about this happening long and hard. It never reoccurred for the rest of my career. A lesson was learnt.

Because of the cancers that patients suffered from, we spent a lot of time taking patients to the X-ray department for their radiotherapy treatments. We would deliver them in a wheelchair and then return to the Ward. Usually about two hours later there would be a phone call asking us to pick the person up.

Often they felt nauseated and exhausted. We had to put creams on the irradiated area, and then encourage fluid intake and a light diet. Cancer seemed to take away appetite and patients were loathe to eat. Generally the treatment was very debilitating, and we would do our best to compensate with rest, care and a good diet.

Other patients needing routine X-rays also had to be taken for investigation, this time we would be required to stay, and help the Radiographer position the subject, and offer care throughout the procedure. This could be time consuming, and some of the Radiographers seemed afraid to get their hands dirty and expected the Nurse to do everything.

There was a mobile X-ray unit that could come onto the Ward for people whom it was dangerous to move.

When you saw this machine arrive you knew that someone was very, very ill.

I saw lots of X-rays and could never interpret them. It amazed me how the Doctors and Radiography staff could see fractures and abnormalities. They meant nothing to me at all no matter how long or hard I looked.

The Ward admitted many patients with inoperable brain tumours, who had become difficult to manage at home.
We had several patients with this terminal condition on the Ward, and they would sit staring into space and completely out of touch. It was very sad. They needed help to eat and drink and steering for every need. It was very hard on their families . Some had surgery but malignant tumours returned and seemed to win every time. It was frustrating for all the Medical and Nursing Staff as we knew that even with the most modern techniques nothing could be done.
One admission was of a very frail young man. His family were with him and after I had clerked him in I packed his case and told his dad to take it home. The man came close and said. "You give my son special care and I will make it worth your while". I was shocked at this attempted bribe, but remained polite and told him his son would get excellent care and there was no need for payment. Sadly the poor boy who had an Astrocytoma (brain tumour) passed the next day.
One patient for admission was a Monk- Brother Johnson. He wore the clothing of his order and had a shaved head. As was usual I took his TPR, Blood Pressure and tested a wee sample. He got into his pyjamas and relaxed in bed. He was very chatty and cheerful and not a bit how I imagined a Monk would be. He exhibited no signs of a brain tumour either and in fact to all appearances had nothing wrong with him.
The Staff Nurse came and told me to go and take my tea break and off I went for half an hour. On my return Angie the Ward Sister called me over.
"Nurse Brown - have you ever done the last offices for a patient?"(this was laying out the dead)
I replied to the contrary and Angie told me to go and lay up a trolley and that I would find a shroud in the Duty room.
I wheeled the trolley to the Sisters Office and the two of us set off. I was pretty sure that the deceased would be one of the staring men, but was incredibly surprised to find it was Brother Johnson.
It seemed that after I admitted him he just lay down in the bed and died. The Doctor had already visited to certify the death and we were to lay him out.
The Brother was still warm and Angie and I started the procedure by saying prayers. He looked like he was asleep and I could not believe that this charming, alert and chatty man had passed so quickly. I was in total shock.
We completed the task, washing the body, closing the eyes, and tying an identifying label on the big toe. We then rang the Mortuary and two Porters arrived to collect the body. They had a special trolley for this with a concealed compartment. The body was placed inside and a sheet draped over. This then looked like an empty trolley and it was taken away, hidden from prying eyes.
I kept thinking about Brother Johnson and wondering how he could possibly have gone from vibrant life to death in half an hour? The most likely explanation was that his tumour had burst a blood vessel and he had died from this. Obviously when your time has come God takes you and you go!
Sister Angie was nice to me in all the things I did offering praise and encouragement. All the Nurses and patients loved her and it was a pleasure to work on her well organised, happy Ward.

We had another patient admitted with severe arthritis. She was rude, demanding and critical of everything done for her.
She had a daughter who was in her late thirties. A single lady, who had devoted her life to caring for this unpleasant mother. She worked and enjoyed this as it must have been an escape from the spiteful harridan.
One of the Doctors suggested that the old lady needed to go into a Nursing home as she had become such a burden. However she had other ideas and decided that her daughter should leave her work and look after her full-time. She was incredibly selfish and clearly thought everyone was put in the world to wait on her, hand, foot and finger . She could not care less about her daughter's quality of life. It was all me, me, me.
One afternoon I was on duty and the daughter of this woman approached me and asked what she should do about her mother? She said that probably she could give up her job for her mother , but was clearly not happy about it. She saw the need for care as a duty and I decided this notion needed removing. Knowing how unpleasant the mother was, and how mean, the last thing the daughter wanted was a nervous breakdown looking after her.
I think inspiration came.

"Now the Doctor has said your mother requires Nursing Home care. She needs two people to move and handle her. It would be incredibly selfish of you to try and do this at home by yourself. You must put your mother first and put her in full- time care. She needs professionals not a well meaning amateur because you would cause pain and suffering"
I impressed on this nice woman that she was not up to the task. I knew if she thought her mother would fare better in care she would go.

My message clearly went home. The following week the nasty old woman was discharged to a Nursing Home and the daughter retained her life. Who knows with such a liability absent she might even have met a nice man and settled down.
I was so pleased at this outcome but did not discuss it with anyone else.

I was now entering my second year of training. I had come a long way and learned all manner of Nursing duties. We were told to go to the laundry room and collect new hats. These were still paper, but had a blue stripe on them to note our status. In another six months we would receive a Petersham belt with the Hospital buckle on it. On the buckle was the Westminster coat of arms and it was a much coveted item.
We all felt proud to have survived that first grinding year. Being the lowest grade of worker and doing the most menial tasks. We now had some respect from our cohorts and were competent in many areas.
Not only that but I had started to enjoy the Nursing. Every day was different and exciting and I was meeting a fascinating panorama of humanity.

One of the Ward patients was a man diagnosed with Leukaemia. He was in his forties and the story told about him was that the family had a Nanny and he had divorced his wife to marry her. Somehow he had got custody of his three children and the Nanny continued to care for them, plus of course other duties.
Each day the Nanny and three quite young children turned up to visit. The patient was going downhill fast but was obviously determined to ignore his illness and get home.
Relentlessly the Leukaemia progressed and the man grew more ill and weaker. Still he hung on. Lacking red blood cells his body was no longer properly oxygenated, and the periphery started to die. Patches of gangrene appeared on his face, and nose. Black weeping sores. There was nothing we could do. He was terminal but was putting up a terrific fight.

The black patches spread to other parts of his body - Fingers and toes. There was a rotten smell in his room as the gangrene made its presence felt. He was very weak and ill but he would not give in.

The Nanny and children continued to visit. A lot depended on this man and he knew it. He was not ready to leave the world, but his time was running out. He refused morphine knowing it would hasten his end. There was nothing more medicine could do for him.

One night he died in his sleep. By this time his nose had gone and his body was covered in sores. It was very sad. I think he left an estate that was a complete mess and now the Nanny had full time child care for 24/7 and she would not even be paid. We never heard the ending of this story but probably the children would be returned to the mother's care and the Nanny would be free to pursue her career.

Another memorable patient was a spinster lady who was just 60 years and a newly retired teacher.

She had some vile cancer and it fungated into the small of her back and presented as a huge sinus.(hole)

Every day a dressing was needed to try and stop pathogens invading the sinus and causing infection.

Often I did this and would get a paraffin and eusol liquid mix and yards of sterile, tube - gauze. The gauze would be soaked in the paraffin fluid and then with forceps packed into the wound. This lady never complained about any pain and had a euphoria and optimism that is peculiar to terminal cancer patients. She talked constantly about a retirement bungalow she had purchased in Devon. She would describe it in detail and speak of the wonderful views in a beautiful landscape. She seemed to have no idea that her days were numbered and she would die in her hospital bed. I knew the medics would have discussed her prognosis with her but she had dismissed this and would happily contemplate a future in the bungalow.

After her dressing was done we would treat her pressure areas and make her as comfortable as possible. She was a lovely lady and you wished something could be done to arrest the blight on her.

A couple of weeks later she did pass. I suppose someone else bought the property and her dream was never realised.

Another patient who was memorable was a bald little man who was placed in a private room. He looked like the' Mekon' from the 'Dan Dare' comic.

He lay in bed naked except for a sheet covering. He had spindly legs and arms, but a huge bloated abdomen. Tubes seemed to sprout out of his body and these drained into large jars under his bed. The man had terminal cancer and had ascites which is copious amounts of fluid in the abdomen. This signals an end stage with the cancer. I was told that this man was very wealthy, and was a PP (Private patient) and was getting a lot of attention from one of the Consultants. He had an IV and was barely conscious. We were told not to do any 'readings' on him, but just to keep an eye.

I checked things out every half hour or so and it was 8.30 pm, half an hour to the end of the shift.

I entered the 'Mekon's' room, and to my amazement he had shrunk. He appeared at half his original size and I noticed that the large jars under the bed were filled with lurid green fluid. It was obvious from the sight of him that he had died, and I went to seek help.

It was a fact that for all his money he could not buy his way out of the cancer curse. He had hung on as long as possible and his end was memorable.

I went off duty so did not see how the 'Laying Out' was dealt with. I presume all the tubes would need removing and the green fluid disposed of. Quite a grim sight, and unpleasant mess to clear up.

Every day on Angie's Ward was a good one and working there was an enjoyable experience. I had more seniority now and we saw the new entry Nurses floundering just as we had done and tried to encourage and help them.
A Notice went up in the Nurses Home inviting my Set to sign up for a three month Obstetric Course at Roehampton Hospital, Maternity Unit.
Chris, Bau and I decided this was something we wanted to do so we added our names to the list.
Bau had just finished a stint on the Opthalmic Ward. This had been a very difficult time for her as she was phobic about eyes and had found the Nursing very testing. The eight week placement had really taxed her and she was relieved it was all over.
Bau had an experience that made us laugh. Many patients were obsessed about their bowel actions and would constantly ask for laxatives. The drug of choice was Sennokot and this was handed out freely with apparently the desired effect. Bau decided she was constipated and took some Sennokot from the Ward to solve her problem. Far from doing this she experienced severe abdominal pain and was laid up for half a day spending a lot of time sitting on the toilet. After this episode you just had to mention the word Sennokot for her to start screaming and ranting. She warned all the patients but to no avail and the demand for the drug was never higher. A lot of old people are bowel fixated and that seemed to be their main topic of conversation in hospital.

Towards the end of my time on Angie's Ward I witnessed serious abuse of a patient.
A very old woman was admitted and she was in a dirty, degenerate condition. It was evening and myself and a third year Nurse were sent to bath her and tidy her up. The third year seemed to be in a bad mood and when we got to the bed with a wash bowl, towels and fresh linen and gown for the patient, she roughly pulled the curtains round the bed. She then removed the covers off the old woman only to discover that she had been doubly incontinent. There was urine and faeces in the bed, a bad mess and bad smell.
We needed tissues to clean her up and I was about to fetch these when the other Nurse exploded in a rage.
"You filthy, disgusting old woman" she shouted. "Look at the mess you have made. Why did you not ask for a bedpan".
Having made this statement she punched the old woman several times until she cried out.
I had never seen patient abuse before and was really shocked to the core.
We cleaned the woman up together with my peer grumbling all the time.
I should have reported this incident to the Ward sister but this Nurse was my senior and we were in a strict line of obedience. In the end nothing was said about this, but it did leave a nasty taste in my mouth. No one was ever told about the incident, but it was a worry, and in my opinion the abuse was totally misplaced and uncalled for.
This was the only time I saw such a thing except for the bad tempered Staff Nurse on the Kids Ward. Most of the Nursing Staff were incredibly, kind and patient. They really cared about their patients and took incontinence and selfish, demanding behaviour in their stride.

One morning as I did the TPR's I noticed that one of the patients was flushed and running a temperature. This lady was post-heart surgery and was on the Ward for convalescent care and recovery.

The findings were reported to the Ward sister and she checked out the patient herself. It was not good and an Oxygen mask was put on, and half hourly observations were ordered.

I was sent off for a mid-morning break and when I returned the patient called Maddy was in an Oxygen tent. Sister Angie was very worried and phoned up the husband to come to the Hospital.

Maddy continued to deteriorate and a lot of Doctors came in to examine her.

Suddenly we were told she was going back to the Operating Theatre for examination and treatment.

Maddy returned with a big drain in her heart. She had an infected heart and the diagnosis was grim. Her poor husband was pacing up and down outside her bed and looked terrified. We learned that there were three young children at home and this did not auger well.

A thick, green/yellow pus drained from Maddy and her condition continued to deteriorate. No more could be done. An IV had been set up and antibiotics were being pumped in but it was too late. Maddy was out of it and with a final gasp she passed away. This whole drama had played out on my shift.

The husband was distraught and kept saying "my children have no mum-what am I to do?" Nothing could be said to comfort him and all the Staff were upset and shocked at this unexpected death.

Sister Angie asked me to prepare a 'Laying Out' trolley as we would do this together. Maddy was only 26 years of age and her operation had been considered to be low risk.

When we got to Maddy behind drawn curtains Sister Angie burst into tears. We were both deeply affected and said prayers as best we could.

The Last Offices were performed and the heart drainage tube was removed. A huge gush of infected pus came out of the drain wound and it was obvious that poor Maddy did not stand a chance of recovery.

It was a truly awful situation for everyone, and although we did not see the husband again I did wonder how the poor man coped?

A teenage girl called Elizabeth came in. She was very pretty and sweet and her father was a doctor. She had renal failure and kidney treatments were in their infancy but dialysis machines had been brought into use in a specialist unit and the girl could have been kept alive by this treatment. On top of that the World' first heart transplant had been performed by Christian Barnard in 1967, and there was increasing talk of kidney transplants that had been done since the 1950's.

The young girl was very ill indeed, but in spite of all the new research the father decided there was nothing to be done and allowed his daughter to die. It was very upsetting, and he must have regretted this decision as within a few months transplantation of the kidney became quite common and was life-saving.

GOING BACK

We were told that after this Ward placement we would have two weeks holiday and I was in a dilemma about what to do and where to go.

I had another letter from Reg and he had invited me to come home for my 'leave'. I really had nowhere else to go. Auntie Dot had not invited me back and I wasn't keen to go to Bexley and to meet up with Geoff because I was so fat.

I now realised that I had put on a colossal amount of weight and needed to do something about it. What was worse, most of my clothes no longer fit and there was no money to buy new. I had to manage with a minimal wardrobe and had a lot of nice things that sat in the cupboard as they no longer fit. Even my smart coat was too tight, and it was all a worry.

I had grown out of my uniform and was at least three sizes larger than when I commenced training. I had to keep going to the sewing room and swop my dresses and aprons for a bigger fit.
Not only that, I was finding my time at work was exhausting as was on my feet for hours on end. There was an urgent need to shed some pounds.

I decided to visit the Nurses Doc and see if he would give me some slimming tablets or something. His reputation told that he was more than generous with prescription drugs and most of the Nurses seemed to be on the birth control pill. Others had done well too so I was optimistic.
Dr Weir was not very sympathetic. He told me the obvious which was to eat less and exercise more. I told him the food we got was stodgy and mooted the idea of the slimming pills. "No! No-way", was his reply to this. He wrote me a letter to the kitchen saying I was on a diet. This resulted in me being given one orange instead of a pudding at lunch on one day, and that was it.
Dr Weir was a very charming man but not a very good doctor. Later in my training I managed to drop a bed on my foot. The foot swelled up and was painful. Dr Weir sent me for an X-ray but there was no follow up so I continued my nursing duties with a crepe bandage and hobbling round. I presumed that there was nothing really wrong.
Some time later, Chris was working on the Nurses sick ward and had access to medical notes. She read mine and said that the X-ray had reported a fracture of my foot and I should have been put in plaster. It did get better eventually, but Dr Weir needed to have been in touch about it.
The Nurses sick ward was a good place to get to. As well as top class Nursing care you got all manner of gourmet food and hot lemon and honey drinks on a regular basis. Mostly the Nurses went in with either flu or burnout. A couple of weeks of pampering usually effected a full cure and back they went to work.
I was never lucky enough to get admitted even though one night I had a bad rigour in my room and called the night sister. I was shaking like a leaf for over an hour, had a high temperature and felt ill. The night sister was unsympathetic and more or less ignored me. Any hope of getting to the Nurses Ward went straight out of the window!

I phoned Hilda and asked to come home for my holiday. She sounded quite pleased to hear from me after nearly a year, but I paid for the phone call. On all the occasions that I rang home, there was never a call back, and the phone swallowed up my sixpences and shillings. Hilda was still mean and cost counted everything.
This going back to the abusive parents was a stupid mistake. If I had reconnected with Nanny Lou she would have taken me in, or it was possible to have done two weeks residential Agency work. However Chris and Bau were both going home so there was subtle pressure to do the same.

I arrived in Lichfield and Reg picked me up from the station in his new car. They were now living in a detached house with three bedrooms on the RAF camp at Fradley. It was another bleak and windswept place and the house was very cold. I was given a 'put- u -up bed', sharing a room with Margaret and that was a bonus as we had a lot to talk about.
We caught up on all the news and Margaret quizzed me about the Nursing. She was 14 now and at Grammar school in Lichfield. She was interested in teaching as a career but also felt that Nursing had its attractions. She told me that Hilda was as tight as ever and they had a really mean lifestyle that was sans everything. Also that the rows were less and the physical abuse had largely stopped. One theory about this was that after Reg's violent Cyprus attack

on me he had been reprimanded by the RAF as this had become public knowledge. A report would have been written and if Reg persisted with this type of behaviour he could have been dismissed from the service and he was now under surveillance.

Hilda had purchased second-hand bikes as Fradley was so isolated and we all went out riding these. The countryside in that area was beautiful and riding the country lanes an enjoyable experience.

One odd thing that happened was that every night as I was going to sleep I felt the bed tip. My feet were lifted up in the air and it seemed like any moment I would fall out. I didn't discuss this but Margaret said this had happened to her too, and it was paranormal and probably one of Hilda's spirits as she was still into the Occult. It was not particularly scary, but I did wonder what was going on.

Amazingly Hilda did not ask me for my board and keep. She never did in all the times I stayed at home. This was very good as I was able to claim back the Nurse's home charges for the two weeks absence and got extra money. Margaret eventually went Nursing too and always got asked for money when she went home so I was really lucky.

There was an uneasy truce between me and my parents. Reg was 40 now and had grown up a bit. He still made me feel sick when he got close and this never left me. The sight of him brought back the cruelty and violence I had suffered.

Hilda was still as mean as could be and totally worshipped money. She seemed calmer but continued to row with Reg about absolute trivia. No one spoke during these rows and Maxine and Margaret seemed really fed up with their lifestyle.

When I got back to London there was a letter telling me that I was to go to Roehampton and start the Obstetric Course. This meant moving Nurse's Homes and going to Roehampton Manor which was the new accommodation. I packed up all my few possessions and caught a bus to the new Hospital.

This Nurse's Home was huge, and my room much better than in London. For a start it was carpeted and warm and there was a plug so I could play my tape-recorder. The downside was that everywhere you went was a long walk. This included the bathroom and the Nurse's kitchen. There were dozens of rooms in this huge building and getting anywhere was a trek. I do not envy anyone living in a huge house as doing even the basics is very hard going. I suppose all the walking is one way of staying fit.

Chris and Bau had also arrived at this home and were both full of their holidays.

Bau had been to Singapore where her family lived and then with her father went to Quebec in Canada for expo 67. She had a wonderful time and said she intended to head off for Canada when qualified. On top of this her dad had offered to buy her a Nursing Home anywhere she liked for her to run and enjoy. The wealth of this family was hard to take on board, especially for someone with my background.

Chris had been back to Ireland and also had a great time. Her parents had given her a cassette recorder and some tapes. This was very 'state of the art', and impressive. It was obvious that both girls had been given a lot of money to sub the poor Nursing wages. However I did get extra that month from the rebated board and lodging charges so I was pleased too.

The Obstetric Course was not to start for another week so I was sent to a General Ward to fill in the time. This Ward was next to the plastic surgery/ burns unit and I felt my future was in this direction. I visited the Ward and a Staff Nurse showed me round. Most of the patients had severe burns and were being 'Barrier Nursed' to reduce the risk of infection. Many were growing skin pedicels and were having a tough time. The most noticeable thing to me was the

terrible smell. The dead, burnt flesh had a horrible odour. It really turned my stomach and I realised that this was not going to be for me.
Roehampton burns unit had a good reputation for excellence and if it had not been for the awful smell it would have been an ideal placement for when I qualified.

LOTS OF GEORGEOUS, TINY BABIES

The Obstetric Course started with a series of lectures. It was a three months stint and included work experience and tuition. If my performance was satisfactory I would get a Certificate at the end of it.

My first placement was on the Ante-Natal Ward. This was fairly relaxed as most of the 'mums to be' were just in for rest and monitoring.
Some were 'social' patients who already had so many kids at home they were run ragged and needed admission to get some rest. Others had Pre-Eclampsia which is a serious condition of pregnancy that mainly affects first time mothers. Rest and monitoring were required and if things did not improve an elective Caesarian was performed.
One woman of Greek nationality had a condition called Hyperemesis Gravidarum (Sickness of pregnancy) and this manifested in non-stop vomiting. I spent ages with her offering sick bowls and glasses of water. Some physicians think this condition has psychiatric reasons with the mother rejecting the pregnancy. This patient was five months gone and the sickness seemed to be of a physical nature. She was discharged after a week or so and she was still puking.
The other thing about this Ward was that it had an Ante-Natal clinic attached to it.
We were required to get experience in this and I found it hard going. Our supervisor called Mary would ask us to examine pregnant women and report on the findings verbally to her. We would palpate the abdomen and locate the baby's head. Or was it the butt? I never knew so always said it was the head. It took someone with experience to feel a breech and everything felt the same to me. As long as I said it was a vertex lie and the head either was or was not engaged (and this was easy to feel) I got away with the clinic. It was all a bit nerve wracking though as Mary seemed to expect a lot for two days lectures but it was the same for all of us.
On top of this we had to check urine specimens looking for sugar or protein. The former indicating diabetes of pregnancy and the latter combined with raised blood pressure Pre-Eclampsia.
There was a lot to learn including listening to the foetal heart.
There was no sonar scan in those days and the Midwifery Staff had to rely on manual palpating and the foetal stethoscope. The babies could not be sexed either and although amniotic sampling could be performed there was not much point as this was prior to the abortion act.
On the Ward we had Rhesus negative mothers who were expected to miscarry. Nowadays injections (Anti D-immunoglobulin) can be given to solve this problem, but not then and some women miscarried many times as they carried a Rhesus positive baby. It was a tragedy but the cause was not fully understood.
It was a bit boring on the Ward and we would see the regular departure of women to the Labour Ward as their babies decided to put in an appearance. Apart from the observations and bed making there was not much to do.
I had started a strict diet on this Ward and was eating only small portions of food and no peanuts or chocolate. I felt exhausted much of the time from low blood sugar but was determined to shed weight.

One day Bau and I who were on the same Ward were sent to fetch a gas and air machine and as we wheeled it to the Ward we decided to try it out. This was nitrous oxide (laughing gas) and we were soon laughing helplessly and giggling after we inhaled it. It took a long while to deliver the machine as we were quite incapable for a bit.

After four uneventful weeks on the Ante-Natal I was transferred to the 'Milk Kitchen' along with another Nurse and here we were required to make up dozens of feeds for the babies from formula. There was a mixing machine and the Night staff had sterilized the bottles, so using several packets we mixed up the feeds and put about 3oz in each bottle. There were several different types of formula and we had to mark out which type they were depending on the mother's preference. We even had a request for a baby that was to be fed on evaporated milk. The format for this was 1oz of evaporated in the bottle topped with two and a half ounces of water and a teaspoon of sugar. It took about four hours to make up all the feeds and these were stored in large fridges. We had loads of empty return bottles to wash and put in hypochlorite to cleanse them. The teats were washed in salt to remove mucous and then also popped into the steriliser. It was a busy production line and there were no disposables in those times. We had to make up bottles of sterile water as well, so that thirsty little mites could get a drink.
I was a week in this kitchen. We must have saved the Hospital a fortune comparing the costs with disposables.

Roehampton was a bit isolated and we were a long way from the village and shops; it seemed to be a quiet place with not much going on.
One afternoon I was in my room when a knock came at the door.
I was just about to take a nap, but opened it and to my surprise a man stood there.
"I'm here to check your electrics", he said. "There are some problems". He was quite a smart looking man but I didn't ask him in.
"There's nothing wrong with my light or plugs " and I switched the light on and off to prove the point.
"OK" he said and I closed the door and didn't think anything further about it.
Half an hour or so later another knock came at my door. This time it was two men.
"We are police" said one of the men.
"Have you had a man call round and ask to check your electrics?"
I agreed this had happened and the policeman told me that this was a burglar and they wanted a description of him. As he was nondescript and I'm not a very observant person, my information was poor, and the police realised there was not much forthcoming so left. One of the police was incredibly good looking and it was a pity he didn't stay longer. It amazed me that a burglar would visit a Nurses Home as most of the girls had very little material goods or money, but obviously thieves are not very fussy!
While there I seemed to be working opposite shifts to Chris and Bau and did not see them very often. I felt quite lonely and apart from enjoying the Obstetric training had little to do in free time and there was no library.
I made friends with an Ethiopian girl called Alice who was doing the SEN (State Enrolled Nurse- A more practical training classed lower than the SRN)
 and claimed to be a member of the Ethiopian Royal Family. She was amusing and had a very relaxed manner in relation to everything. She was working on a General Ward and would tell highly amusing stories about her patients and had us all in fits of laughter.
One day she invited Bau, Chris and self to tea and said she would make us a traditional Ethiopian meal which we would love. We duly turned up to her room at 3pm and with great ceremony served us the meal. The food mainly seemed to be mashed up bread with curry

powder in it. It was horrible and not liking to seem rude or ungrateful we tried to tuck in. None of us ate much and Alice had a huge bowl of the mashed up bread. After a couple of hours we were able to leave without giving offence. Any hopes of an exotic feast were well and truly dashed, but the meal was memorable, probably for the wrong reasons.

After the week in the Milk Kitchen I was transferred to the Labour Ward.
We had lectures on Childbirth and what was involved and our role was mainly to assist the midwives and Doctors and observe and learn.

There are three stages of Labour. The first is when the contractions start at the end of the pregnancy. The usual time is 40 weeks gestation but frequently it is shorter but it can go 2 or 3 weeks over the optimum time.
Sometimes the contractions were practice ones and the Labour was false, (Braxton-Hicks contractions). The First Stage could be as long as 48 hours and was markedly so in a first timer. A lady having subsequent babies was usually a lot quicker and this all had to be allowed for.
Once the cervix (neck of the womb) had fully dilated the Second stage started. This was the time that the mother had to start pushing the baby out in a rhythm with her contractions. 20 minutes was allowed for the Second stage and if no baby was forthcoming emergency deliveries were done. The Third stage was the delivery of the placenta. All this was explained in our school lectures and now on the Ward I was going to see the process in action.

The women in Labour were obviously in a lot of pain but we were told Pethidine or other analgesics were not to be used as they affected the baby, depressing respiration. The only drug regarded as safe was the gas and air (nitrous oxide)
And this is what the women got. While in Labour we would measure the rate of contractions, keep a check on the foetal heartbeat and the midwife would do internal examinations to measure the stretching of the cervix as the baby's head came down. As long as all the readings were OK the mum was allowed to progress to a 'normal delivery', but regular observations every quarter of an hour were made.
We were told in school that there was no such thing as a 'normal delivery' except in retrospect.
We were on the alert with the women as things could progress or change very quickly, and sometimes did.
I saw my first birth on my very first day on the Ward. It was fascinating. The lady giving birth was a' primip' (first timer) and was pretty well on top of things. She co-operated well with the midwife and her baby was born quickly. The midwife had to cut her perineum (episiotomy) to stop tearing into the urethra that could cause chronic incontinence later.
The sight of the baby emerging into the world was amazing. This white, plastic, bundle of flesh would appear, a huge gasp of air and in a trice a pink, wriggling baby was there as if by magic. The umbilical cord was cut and the baby wrapped and put in the mother's arms. Labels were made and attached to the baby's ankle. These had the family surname and mother's hospital number on it. This was very important and was double checked like giving drugs.
After the birth we awaited the delivery of the placenta. This was carefully scrutinized by the midwife as if parts were retained it could cause haemorrhage and severe post-natal complication. If bits of placenta were left behind the mother would need surgery to remove them.

As this mum had an episiotomy we had to wait for the Doctor to come and stitch her. The midwife was not allowed to do this although nowadays they probably do. A midwife was allowed to put up an IV that was banned to other Nurses and again this is all changing.
The baby was examined by the midwife for any obvious defects and an APGAR score given. (Appearance, pulse, grimace, activity and respiration) The expected rate was 8-10 and lower than this put the staff on the alert and if under 6 the baby was rushed to Special Care. This particular baby was fine and scored 9 so all was well.

At this point the new father was brought in to greet his wife and new son. Dads were not encouraged in the delivery room then, although they can be a great help and support to their wives, and it was a mistake to exclude them.
Once it was established the mum was not bleeding or any problems she and the baby were taken to the post-natal Ward and it was my job to clear up the delivery room. We wore gowns for the delivery and these went to the laundry. Instruments were returned to the CSSD (Central services sterile department) for recycling, and the waste materials from the Labour dressing packs thrown away. Nothing was saved that could not be sterilised to prevent the risk of cross infection. Mothers were at high risk of infection after the birth and all staff had to ensure that maximum protection was offered. The room and delivery bed had to be swabbed down with disinfectant and the cleaner was summonsed to wash the floor. The rooms were kept clean to operating theatre standards and the mother's safety was an absolute top priority at all times.
Unfortunately the Staff on the Labour Ward were not very pleasant. One midwife was called Jones the bitch. She was nasty to everyone including the mothers and showed no sympathy for the excruciating pain of childbirth and was abrupt and rude to everyone. The Registrar who dealt with the Forceps deliveries and Caesars was also a nasty man. He was vulgar and coarse and unpleasant to have around.
One day I was on duty in the Labour Ward with Jones the bitch and a woman in heavy labour was admitted. She was helped onto a bed in the reception room and Jones did an internal examination to assess progress and estimate cervical dilation. She's only 5 centimetres she said. The woman groaned as another contraction came, and Jones told me to do an internal as well. I estimated full dilatation and told Jones. "What a load of rubbish" said Jones and went to get a wheelchair to take the mother to the Labour Ward. The woman let out a scream and started to push. Seconds later the baby's head emerged. Jones went to pieces. She started shouting and gibbering and her words were "don't panic" which she repeated over and over. The baby was now out and I ran for a delivery pack. We managed to sort things and Jones calmed down eventually. The mum was fine. No perineal tears or need for stitching and she and the baby were good with normal placental delivery. This was the mum's third baby (a 'multip') and Jones should have listened to me when I told her that we had full dilatation and delivery was imminent.
Another lady who I cared for had a very long hard Labour. She was past her 40 weeks dates by nearly a fortnight and was being induced with an Oxytocin drip. Things were not going well and little was happening. The woman was not coping and seemed to be almost hysterical, and screamed every time she had even the smallest contraction. She was abnormally anxious about the baby and was generally agitated.
At long last her contractions speeded up and delivery became close. She was taken into the delivery room and helped to push the baby into the world. The baby took its first gasp and that was OK. It was a little girl but was very odd looking and had a pixie type face. "Is my baby alright?" shrieked the mother.
The midwife did not reply and the mother repeated her question. I thought the baby looked cute and said "yes, she's fine and really sweet".

The midwife did not give the baby to the mother but rushed it out to Special Care. The mother became even more hysterical and started yelling and demanding to see her baby. The midwife said she could see the child later.

The baby had William's syndrome. This gives a pixie like appearance to the face and is associated with mental retardation and cardio-vascular problems. It's a very rare congenital abnormality. The child would be difficult to rear and maybe there was a good reason for the mother's heightened tension prior to giving birth.

On one of the deliveries, also a first timer, the husband insisted on being present at the birth. His wife was in an advanced stage of labour and was wheeled into the delivery room. The midwife made the husband gown up with shoe covers and a mask, and he sat next to his wife to help and observe the proceedings.

It was not an easy labour and the lady found the contractions very painful, she was given gas and air but this did not seem to be helping much.

Finally the midwife did an examination and said that we had full dilatation and on the next contraction the mother needed to push.

Off we went with the midwife feeling for contractions and then telling the mother to push down hard. It was obviously all very painful and the pusher was not doing very well."Come on "said the midwife" Or we will be getting the forceps out, Push, push, push"

The mother made a rather feeble effort and again the midwife encouraged her "Come on now, try a lot harder" a bit more pushing happened with plenty of grunting and gasping. The husband was getting agitated and decided to join the action.

"Come on darling push, push" he said.

There was a silence for a few seconds and then his now red in the face wife turned round to face him, "You bloody push" she shouted and at the same time cracked him hard round the face.

The poor man looked stunned but seconds later the baby's head appeared. Obviously the effort had done the trick. Both the midwife and I were trying not to laugh and the arrival of a dear little baby boy kept us busy and in control.

I presume the couple made this little altercation up as it all happened in the heat of the moment!

No matter how many deliveries I saw the wonder of each birth was impressive. Each child born was special and beautiful and the birth a total wonder. It was all truly amazing and a privilege to be present. You really got to see the hand of God as each little miracle took its first breath.

I never did a delivery myself although Bau did and was excited and enthusiastic about her experience. Although Roehampton was not a Midwifery training school, it was a place for Medical students to get experience and mostly they got to do the deliveries. There was always keen competition to assist with the birthing process.

As well as normal deliveries we got to see what happened when things went wrong.

One poor lady was admitted at 32 weeks gestation (term is 40 weeks) with severe Pre-eclampsia. Her blood pressure was sky high and she had swollen legs, albuminuria and terrible headaches. There was fear for her, and the baby, and the only choice left to the medics was a Caesarian Section.

The Operating theatre was made ready and I was told to go and help.

Mainly this meant running around, passing equipment, and doing whatever was required. A Paedriatrician was on hand for the baby and the mother was given a general anaesthetic and in due course a small, red, tiny baby was delivered by surgery. A weak little cry emitted from the baby and after cutting the cord it was weighed and popped into an incubator which was wheeled off to the Special Care unit.

The mother was stitched and returned to the Ward. She made a good recovery and the Pre-Eclampsia disappeared. The baby weighed in at three and a half pounds which is compatible with survival. Babies were kept in the hospital until they reached five pounds in weight and mothers were encouraged to express breast milk for them. Especially the first portion, which is the Colostrum, and full of anti-bodies. Once the mum had gone to the Post-Natal Ward we lost contact but at that time even a baby of 26 weeks could be reared.

A Forceps delivery was horrific. This was done when the mother reached the second stage of labour and for some reason obstructed. This might be an abnormal foetal position, a very large baby, or the mother's exhaustion. It was not pleasant to watch. The mother had a huge perineal cut made and the two forceps which were like big spoons were put on the baby's head and traction (pulling) was applied. The poor little mites were usually born with bruising to the face and head but the second stage of Labour is a critical time with a 20 minute window only to get the baby out or there is a high risk of foetal death.

Seeing this procedure was enough to put anyone off childbirth for life. Years later this did happen to me and the pain was terrible. I remember thinking at the time "Thank God I can't see what's happening".

The Labour Ward was stressful and unpredictable. I was glad to have had the experience and found the birth process fascinating.

The next slot was the Post-Natal Ward. Busy with all the new mums and babies. Some were first timers and needed a lot of support. Even normal deliveries were kept in for a week or more and Caesarians a fortnight.

We did TPR's on all the mothers and watched for any raised temperatures to show infection. The lochia (discharge) was checked and we measured the involution of the uterus (shrinking) to ensure normal progress. If there was retained placenta this would not go to plan and the mother would be taken to Theatre and a clear out done under anaesthetic.

Mums who were breast feeding needed support and encouragement. Although we were only Second Year Nurses we were expected to offer mums expert advice on feeding and infant care. The bottle fed babies were easier to monitor as at least you could see what they were getting.

As well as the feeding we had to clean the umbilical stump with surgical spirit, and make sure there was no infection. The resolution of the cord was by dry gangrene. It gave no pain to the baby but sometimes they could be sticky.

We would weigh the babies and chart progress (usually there was initial weight loss). On top of this we would do nappy changes and check that meconium (first stools- a black tar like substance) was passed and there was no blockage. All the babies had a medical check from the Paedriatrician and most of them were fine. Occasionally there would be a heart defect or other problem and these babies were transferred to specialist units.

While on this Ward a French woman was delivered and it was thought that her baby had 'Downs Syndrome'. Blood was taken for genetic testing and the baby who was a poor feeder remained in a care cot. The mother had four other children but seemed to take an interest and after her discharge would return to see the baby. Finally the results of the Chromosome test came back. The 'Downs Syndrome' was confirmed. The mother was told, and she stopped her visits and abandoned the baby. I found this to be shocking but there was nothing to be done and the baby was to be put up for adoption.

For some reason Bau took against this baby and sympathised with the mother. I have always found children with this condition loving, friendly and attractive. It was unbelievable that such a situation could happen. There is increased risk of this condition in the child as the mother gets older.

I was doing nights on this Ward and one evening we had a Caesar patient returning from theatre late. Things had not gone well with the delivery and the midwife who brought her back told me about the problems and said to watch her carefully as there was a high risk of haemorrhage. The patient's baby had gone to special care and her husband and parents were with her.
"Please look after her Nurse" said the husband to me. "She's had a really rough time".
I assured the anxious family we would watch her and set up quarter hourly observations. There were only two Nurses on duty-me and a West Indian midwife. The latter did the drug round and I covered the rest. It was pretty busy as I fed the bottle babies and changed them, and wheeled in the breast fed from the Nursery. The midwife seemed to have disappeared and the night wore on. I kept up observations on the Caesar and all was well. The midwife suddenly showed up at about 3 am and told me to go off for my meal break. Before going I explained that the Caesar needed quarter hourly observations and was high risk of bleeding. Having done this went for my meal and break.
I returned at 4am only to find the midwife asleep at the Nurses station. I rushed to the Caesar. No observations had been done and when I took the pulse it was fast, weak and thready. I pulled back the sheets and sure enough there was a lot of blood. I immediately raised the bed (emergency procedure) and alarm to get help. Things did not look good, but swift action followed and the woman was rushed to Theatre and 'packed' to stop the bleeding.
After the fuss was over I went back to the woman's bed and noticed that all the missing observations had been written in. I know that if I had not been vigilant we would have lost the patient that night.

Mary the midwifery Superintendant gave us lectures and was very pleasant. She was only young, and generated enthusiasm and excellence.
One of the Nurses told her that the Registrar Doctor was doing episiotomies without anaesthetic. She got really angry about this information and said she would sort it out. The next day on the Post -Natal Ward I saw her taking the Doc to task, and she really shouted at him. He was a callous man of Italian origin and his standards were not all one would wish for. I think things did improve after this episode. It must have been very painful for the mothers being cut without anaesthetic.
The three months was up and we all took an examination. We also were marked for our performance on the Unit. I came out top and was very pleased and we all got a Certificate stating that we had completed the course and had spent qualifying time on practice and study. This Certificate was to be very useful to me later on when I sought further training as a Health Visitor.

I had remained on my diet throughout the course and everyone said I had noticeably lost weight. I got on scales on the Ward and saw I weighed over 12 stones and was so upset stupidly decided I was wasting my time, and came off the diet. If only the weight had been charted at the outset, the lost weight would have been an incentive to carry on. I felt and looked better so what utter folly to abandon the effort!

We were all sent back to London and the Nursing school. There was plenty to learn and we had two weeks of short days and weekends free.

The content of the lectures was more advanced. We were taught how to catheterise a patient and the complications with this. How to nurse a patient with pneumonia, and adjunct information like postural drainage, and how to manage a pleural drain.

There was a lot of new stuff to be taken on board and all the girls eagerly took in the new learning, and were prepared for more responsibility on the Wards.

I was living back in the Queen Mary Nurses home in the same wretched room as before.

As we weren't working weekends I accepted an invitation to a party. I went with Chris and Bau and met a young and pleasant South African man. We chatted and got on well and he asked me to go back to his flat with him for a drink. The party was very noisy and there was no food and you had to bring your own drink or go without. It was getting late and I should have gone home but foolishly I agreed to his invitation.

The flat was located in South Kensington and as soon as we got there the young man- Alan turned into a wolf. He put off all the lights in the empty lounge and prepared for major smooching. I hardly knew him and was wondering how to get away and back home. Things were just getting hairy when the lounge door burst open, and one of Alan's flat mates barged in. He switched on the light and Alan immediately jumped up yelling for him to turn it off. This did not happen, and in fact a volley of abuse rang out.

Alan jumped up with fists clenched and a huge, violent fight ensued. This involved ornament breakage and the two men punching and hitting each other. The fight lasted for over ten minutes and both assailants had bloody noses and in Alan's case a black eye and concussion. The other guy stormed off and Alan collapsed on the couch. I helped to clean off the blood and looking at the clock saw it was after midnight. The Nurses Home would be locked and if I was seen out would be in a lot of trouble.

Alan fell sound asleep on the couch. I had to sit there until 6am and then crept out of the flat and went to find a bus. I had to walk miles to get a ride home and returned just as the Nurses Home door opened. After creeping in, and getting to my room, managed to sleep as it was Sunday.

It was a big relief to be back and that was the last party ever attended while I was nursing. Such an event was not my idea of a party anyway. It was typical of the 'Swinging Sixties' that a gathering with no refreshment or entertainment was called a Party. It was pretty obvious that with the sexual revolution of 'The Pill', this sort of mingling was for one purpose only.

Telephone messages arrived from Alan but I never answered them and wanted nothing more to do with him. The whole night was a vile memory.

I visited my Aunty Dot at this time and had Sunday lunch with the family. She was always busy, and had found herself a good job in Market Research. I did a couple of interviews for her whilst there, and returned to the hospital with free samples of biscuits and talcum powder as a reward. I was very pleased. It was nice to catch up with her family. She was very tactful and did not comment on my weight, and I was pleased not to bump into Geoff.

When the fortnight at the school was over our new postings were up and I was to go back to Roehampton to the Men's Orthopaedic ward. My friends were staying in London so would be on my own. This was not very well received. It was the first time I had no support and was very worried about this three month placement that was looming.

Shortly after I arrived alone in Roehampton it was my birthday. I was 20 and spent it entirely on my own.
No cake but a bar of chocolate. I again had no card or gifts from my family and with no friends around there were no celebrations. I spent the day feeling upset and abandoned and was glad when it was over. I was particularly short of cash at the time and decided I could not afford the two or three shillings to ring Hilda, and there was no chance of being called back by Mrs Mega Miser!

I was living back in the Manor House Nurses Home and appreciated the nice room after the London dump. It was a pity there was so much walking, even to get to the bathroom but in the end you did get used to it.
Alice was still around so I befriended her as Bau and Chris were in London.
We chatted a lot and from the sound of it Alice was planning to return to Ethiopia where she would become top Nurse and run all the hospitals. She was good fun and my only social life.

BROKEN BONES

The Men's Orthopaedic Ward was run by a Sister Finnegan and had about 40 beds. It was busy and many of the patients were long stay with broken limbs and pulleys, whilst others with broken backs were confined to body castes.
I took an instant liking to Sister Finnegan. She was small and thin with a huge 'birds nest' of hair, and never walked but seemed to run everywhere. I learned that the 'birds nest' was in fact a wig, as Sister Finnegan had been in a Japanese Prisoner of War Camp in Singapore, and due to the terrible conditions she was subjected to, had lost her hair. Rumour had it that she came to the UK to nurse rather than her home country of Australia to avoid contact with Japanese people, as she now had such an aversion to them.
She was very hard working and focused, and all her nurses had admiration and respect for her.
It was a really good work environment and I enjoyed my three months stay.
There was a lot of care needed for the patients as many were bed bound and needed assistance with all the basics. Bed bathing, regular pressure area care, and bed pans and bottles. Many could not get up at all and had to take their meals and drinks in the bed.
There were some elderly people, but many were quite young and had been in road traffic accidents, or had falls and now needed to be put in plaster and immobilised.
One young man that I took a dislike to was in a full body caste. He had broken his back in a road accident and the story ran that he was with his fiancée who had ended their engagement. They were in his car and he deliberately ran it into a wall at speed. The fiancée was killed outright and he broke his back and was in hospital but would be going to Court when he was better to answer charges pertaining to the death.
He was arrogant, demanding and oddly enough a favourite with some of the Nurses.
One of these fans was a very butch Staff Nurse. She fawned on him and nothing was too much trouble as long as someone else did the work. This man, called Peter, was always wanting attention of some sort, and for some reason consumed vast quantities of bananas.

One day he asked me to get him a bed pan. Not only did he pass piles of stinky stools but you had to clean his bum as he could not reach it. I was very busy at the time but got the pan and placed it under him, drew the bed curtains, and off I went.

A few minutes later his bed light went on and he had obviously finished. Just at that moment the butch Nurse arrived and saw the light. Immediately she was all concern."What's the matter with Peter", she demanded. For once I was quick off the mark. "I'm not sure" I said, "but he's been asking for you".

Immediately she rushed off to serve her pet, who was hidden behind drawn curtains. No doubt she was met with a foul stench and a pan full of poop. I'm sure she was really cross to have been set up to clean him up as she was lazy and seldom soiled her hands. I was at the other end of the Ward giggling at this stage and felt that they deserved each other.

I became adept at avoiding him but he was in the hospital for months and always made his presence felt.

One amusing Nurse on the Ward was an SEN called Sue. She was kind and caring but not ever so bright.

The orthopaedic Consultant was called Mr Smith. He was arrogant, overbearing and made Sister Finnegan's life a misery. He was very demanding and if things were not to his liking he would shout abuse and become very unpleasant. He obviously thought a lot of himself although it was rumoured that he came from a very humble background.

One day Mr Smith turned up on the Ward to do a 'Round'. With a collection of Medical students, the Registrar and Houseman plus Sister Finnegan-every patient was visited and passed judgement on. During this time a hush was imposed on the Ward, all patients were to be in bed and no curtains drawn.

Nurse Sue had a patient on a bedpan and asked for help to get him off. I went to her assistance and realised she did not know that the 'Round' was in progress as we were behind curtains. She started to speak in a loud, slow voice - A voice that could be heard all over the Ward, and certainly by Mr Smith and his entourage.

"I don't like that Mr Smith" said Sue.

"There's something about him I can't take to. I don't know what it is but I really don't like him" Sue thought for a bit after making this statement and then added" He's common, that's what he is".

Such an insult coming from the likes of Sue was hilarious and it was obvious that Mr Smith had heard her as he looked furious. Totally oblivious to the effect that she had Sue sailed forth, clutching the bedpan and made for the sluice. Hardly able to contain my laughter I pulled back the curtains and followed Sue hoping that the Consultant would not see me in fits of giggles.

I met my first Male Nurse on this Ward. His name was Bob and he spent a lot of time in the Staff toilet having a cigarette. He did as little work as he could get away with and didn't stand for any truck with difficult patients. His laid back attitude was amusing and later I realised that although he seemed a bit idle he had been nursing for years and could not be expected to work at a frenetic pace at his age.

At this stage I decided I preferred nursing women. Men actually seemed to complain more and also made little effort towards their rehabilitation and discharge. I was in the minority with this viewpoint and most Nurses preferred to work with the men.

We frequently had diabetics on the Ward with complications and had two old men in beds next to each other- each with gangrene from diabetes. Both had been in before and had below knee amputations on one leg. Now the foot on the other leg was affected and they were scheduled for surgery.

For some reason the two men took against each other, and they spent much of the day bickering and arguing. Over a few days this spatting got more and more aggressive and they were swearing and shouting at each other.

Sister Finnegan had them moved a distance away to separate them but this did not stop the hostility. They now shouted abuse down the ward. Both must have expended a lot of energy on this feud as neither was at all well.

Surgery day arrived for one of the men and whist he disappeared to the theatre peace reigned. On his return he was pretty poorly and out of it. Again there was quiet with no aggressive repartee. This went on for a couple of days and then he surfaced enough to start shouting again and the war of words resumed. After two days of this the second man was due for surgery but that very night, unexpectedly his sparring partner died.

The shouting stopped as the deceased's body was wheeled out of the Ward. The other man went quiet and now there was no one to argue with. That night he too unexpectedly died, and he did not even get his surgery. Somehow it seemed that the rows were keeping them going and when nature called a truce these two adversaries just faded away.

There was a Residential Home near Roehampton for disabled people. It had a very good reputation for care and sometimes we had one of their residents in for treatment.

One man came in and Sister Finnegan said "Oh no! Not him again"

The man was admitted into a private room and his diagnosis was 'For Investigation'.

He was a total pest. He had some sort of spasticity and made constant jerking (Athetoid) movements. He whined and complained about everything that was done for him, and his room alarm light was on constantly as he demanded this and that.

Nothing was ever right. His porridge was cold at breakfast, his bed was uncomfortable, he needed more light and the room was not big enough. His complaints were endless and all the Staff rapidly got fed up with him.

Every morning I would make his bed with another Nurse and he demanded fresh linen on a daily basis. He was quite capable of walking about and would sit in a chair whilst we were working and make critical remarks. He really was most unpleasant and it soon became obvious that his stay on the Ward was to give the Staff in the Residential Home a much needed break from him.

He seemed to be with us forever, and I began to despair that we would be rid of him. No diagnosis had been made although he had run the full gamut of tests. One morning during report, Sister Finnegan said that I needed to strip his bed and sort the room, as Mr Nuisance was being discharged and a new patient coming in.

I took a first year Nurse with me to strip and disinfect the bed and while we were doing this the man started being rude. "I suppose you selfish Nurses are glad I'm going. The care and attention I've had here has been very poor. You all need reporting to management" he droned on for a bit, and by this time we were taking the mattress cover off.

"I bet you're pleased I'm going" said the man.

Both the first year and myself collapsed laughing when he said this. We fell onto the bed in hysterics and he started shouting and cursing us. The more he did this the more we laughed. We could hardly stand up and we eventually both had to leave the room as we could no longer do anything. We agreed to finish the room when he was gone.

About half an hour later I saw a Porter with Mr Nuisance in a wheelchair being taken out of the Ward. He saw me and shook his fist. This resulted in more giggles from me and now I was able to go and get the room sorted. I think every Staff on the Ward was pleased to see the back of him. I felt terribly sorry for the people at the Home where he resided. He must have made everyone's life a misery.

One evening Sister asked me to get a bed ready for a Casualty admission. "It's a broken arm and collarbone"
The patient was brought in on a trolley and was crying, groaning and very precious to say the least." These queers are all the same" said Sister Finnegan, and it was a sign of the times that I had not the faintest idea what she meant.
I helped him get into bed. He had apparently come off a motorbike and his leather jacket was with him. His shirt had been partly cut off and he was in a plaster and wore a sling. He would not co-operate with undressing although I managed to get his pants off and got to view a very odd, red, satin thong that he was wearing. In the end I got scissors and cut off the rest of the shirt and put a hospital gown on him.
We gave him a shot of Pethidine as he appeared to be in so much pain and as my shift finished I left the Ward to the sound of his yells and groans.
The next day when I came on duty after lunch he had gone home. He was the most pathetic man I had ever nursed.

However not all patients put on a brave face in response to pain and stress. British men try to do the stiff upper lip bit but not so other nationalities.
A Greek man was admitted for amputation of a leg. He had circulatory problems and was getting peripheral gangrene. He was quite young, only in his forties. Surgery was duly performed and he was returned to his bed. For a few days we gave him strong painkillers and bandaged his stump with fresh dressings. On the fifth day the Doctor said we should help him to get up and sit him in a chair.
I was designated to do this with another staff. We explained to the patient what was going to happen and lined the chair up. Both nurses took an arm each and heaved to get him into the chair. The man let out a bloodcurdling scream, and then burst into floods of tears. He point blank refused to move. It was important to get him up as very shortly a prosthesis (artificial limb) would be fitted to his stump and he would be helped to walk.
No matter what we said he refused to move. In the end we gave up and went and informed the Sister about our problem.
She was very nice about this and with a Staff Nurse went to do the job herself.
Terrible screams rang out from behind the drawn curtains round the man's bed. Five minutes later we saw that the patient had been got out of bed and was sitting in a chair crying.
I think this must have been Greek culture because apart from the 'queer'
I never saw such behaviour in a British man.
Roehampton was famous for making artificial limbs and no doubt this patient was kitted out with a false leg and got walking again.

I seemed to do a lot of night duty on this Ward and if there was one thing I disliked it was the EMSU's. (Early morning specimens of urine)
These would be collected by the Nurses and lined up in the sluice for testing. In the early hours of the morning the smell and sight of this wee turned my stomach. All the results had to be charted and sometimes we would find sugar indicating a diabetic, or protein showing an infection or kidney disease. We reported only. Diagnosis was for the medics and all the Staff had to play their part. Junior Nurses seldom addressed doctors and even when you helped a Doctor with a procedure they largely ignored you and there were no pleases or thank yous. Mainly the Sisters and Staff Nurses interacted with Doctors, and we trainee Nurses seemed to be invisible.
We had a lot more to do with the medical students who would often ask questions and the location of patients who needed blood taken. There was no phlebotomist in those days and all blood tests were done by either Doctors or Medical students.

Some of the Medical students were a bit childish and would pinch my bottom when they had the chance. I ignored them as thought this behaviour was pathetic. Nowadays am sure this does not happen or the scream of 'Sexual Harassment' would be heard.
Society in those days was not litigious and the only representation for Nurses was a useless College of Nursing which happily presided over low wages, exploitive hours and low standards of staff welfare. Not only that, but they made no strides to upgrade the status of Nurses and there were no degree courses. A Diploma in Nursing was in its early stages and had arrived about 20 years too late. The Westminster Hospital did not offer this advanced educational route and it tended to be confined to two, top London teaching hospitals only. We all used to moan about how hard and mean the training was but nothing was ever done. I found the lack of money very difficult and at Roehampton was unable to do the Agency work or get out overnight so I was back to a minimal income.

One patient who made his presence felt was a young man called Toby who was in the Navy and was having his arm tattoos removed. There was no Laser in those days and in this case the skin was removed and a graft put on. This graft was done by growing skin from another area and attaching it to the excised tattoo bed. In this case the arm was anchored to his chest and a piece of skin was growing on the excised tattoo wound. This procedure meant a long stay in Hospital, and Toby was bored, bed bound, and had become a Nuisance
His favourite occupation was trying to put his hand up the Nurses skirt. He was a bit limited in his reach and was possible to avoid. It was very annoying but he thought everyone was fair game-except the Sister of course. He would laugh and shout whenever he scored and I did my best to avoid him. He had the tattoos done while he was a Rating but had been promoted to Officer and no longer wanted them. He was fortunate to get this cosmetic surgery and care on the NHS and should have been in a private hospital and paying. He was still in his bed when I left the Ward and did not seem a bit grateful for his free treatment.

A man was admitted to the ward with skin cancer. I don't know why he came on the Orthopaedic Ward but he turned up one day and I did his admission. He was to be examined by the Doctor so after doing the usual TPR etc I got a hospital gown and told him to undress and put it on. This is where I got my first look at the cancer and what a shocker that was. The growth was under his left arm and it was enormous - a huge pink, sponge like tumour that stretched from his armpit, to just above his waist. It was obvious that no help had been sought by the man and it had been allowed to grow unchecked into this huge mass.
Skin cancer of this type is one of the most successful to treat and surgery was planned to excise the cancer.
All went to plan and the Doctors saw him and he was scheduled for surgery in the coming days. Like all patients there were pre-operative tests to be done and blood work.
One afternoon a medical student turned up and told me he had come to take blood from this man and he went to the bed and drew the curtains. He should have taken about five minutes, but twenty minutes later the curtains were still drawn and I sensed that something was wrong. I went and peeped behind the curtains to be met with a horrific sight. There was blood all over the floor and bed and the Medical student wielding a scalpel.
"What on earth are you doing I shouted" the Medic said" I couldn't find a vein so am doing a cut-down"
This was a major, major error and this procedure was only ever done on moribund patients and then in an extreme emergency. The patient looked understandably frightened not to mention the pain he was being given. I really didn't know what to do next but the next moment I spotted the Registrar and ran to get him. Having blurted out the problem he ran to the bedside and some shouting emerged from behind the curtains. The Registrar took the

blood and asked for a dressing and stitch pack as he tried to repair the wounds and damage done. This was a dreadful incident and I presume the Medical Student was reprimanded but I never heard any more and of course it was my job to clear up the horrible mess left. Mostly Medical Students were closely supervised and I can't help but wonder if this particular one had just learnt about 'cut downs' and wanted to try it out?

Nowadays the patient would have rightly sued the hospital for compensation, but nothing happened as I was never called as material witness to this abuse.

I had started to put on weight again having come off my diet. Christmas was coming and I was working over the holiday and as we had a kitchen I decided to cook myself a turkey. This was pretty stupid, but I went ahead and did it anyway. The turkey came out well but it was far too big for me to eat and even though Alice and I had cold meat and sandwiches most of the carcass had to be binned.

Christmas on the Ward was very quiet. A lot of the patients were sent home and we had minimal work.

Sister Finnegan was on duty much of the day and obviously loved being there. A choir came from the local Church and performed for the patients. It was magical and lifted the whole atmosphere. There was no special Nurses meal like we had the previous year, and my Christmas dinner was eaten in the Staff dining room. There were no gifts or cards for me and the only extra I had was the turkey!

I telephoned Hilda and Reg for a chat. I didn't get to talk to my sisters which was my objective and as my mean parents never rang me back was considerably out of pocket for the long-distance call. Both my birthday and Christmas were a disappointment at Roehampton and I did feel very much alone when I was off duty.

Somehow the three months slipped by and I was notified that my time at Roehampton was over and I was returning to work in London at the Vauxhall Hospital which was located near the Westminster.

I can't say I was sorry to be leaving Roehampton. The hospital was isolated and the Nurses Home miles away from shops or any amenities and although the experience and work were interesting I was glad to get away.

Back in London I was told to visit the laundry room to pick up my navy blue, Petersham belt with the Hospital buckle. This was a sign that I was half way through my training, and marked status on the Ward. All my set got these and were very proud of them. We were told that if we worked our Post-Graduate year for the hospital they would be ours to keep.

My belt was already a bit tight and I realised that if I put any more weight on it would not fit. As it was the strain on the belt ruined the clasp for the buckle and I ended up having to improvise with a safety pin.

I returned again to Queen Mary's Nurses Home and back to the same room. I began to think it was kept empty just for me. Maybe with the noise and crappy view others complained so it was always available.

THREE MONTHS OF HELL

The Vauxhall Hospital dealt mainly with bowel complaints, and I was to go onto the Surgical Ward for another three month stint.

My first day of work set the tone for the duration. I met the Ward Sister who was quite young, blonde and pretty, but she obviously took an instant dislike to me, and was rude and sarcastic in her address.

Maybe she did not like me having bleached, blonde hair as well but my whole stay on this ward was heavy graft topped by a critical and unfair report at the end.

The Ward was one long corridor with beds down each side. The Patients came in for various treatments. A lot of cancer and chronic bowel disease like Crohn's and Ulcerative colitis, where gut resection was needed to try and control the illness.

Because of this we had lots of colostomy and illeostomy care and generally there was an all pervading smell of excreta.

This Ward was extremely busy and every shift was really hard work. As well as acute surgical we had patients with chronic problems that came in for a very long stay.

Like Sister Ball this Ward Sister whose name was Rita was big on cronyism and had her favourite patients and Nurses. She spent most of her time in the Office which I was glad about because when she did emerge to visit some little pet of a patient she would find fault with everything you did.

I really disliked her but was totally under her direction and control. I was more self-confident than previous and tended to be a bit rude and answered her back. This did not go down at all well and she would shun me in the Office report and blame me for anything that went wrong. Overall this placement was an unmitigated disaster.

There were two main Consultants on this Ward, both Surgeons and twice a week they would operate on patients.

This kept us pretty busy with prepping patients and then the aftercare.

A lot of patients had to have bowel clear outs prior to surgery and we would take them downstairs to a special suite for colonic lavage. This would get them ready as in some cases because of rectal cancer, all the lower end of the gut and rectum would be removed. These poor people would then have a permanent colostomy made and we would need to teach the patient how to care for it.

At least with a colostomy the waste passed was solid, and not too smelly. The illeostomies were awful and liquid waste was excreted. The smell was terrible and the collecting bags frequently leaked. Even then we did have disposables and this made the whole process of management easier. Because of the cost of these a lot of illeostomy patients came in with rubber bags that they used at home. The use of them must have been very difficult and keeping oneself smelling clean and fresh, challenging to say the least.

People with these ostomies needed help with skin care as the faeces that was discharged had digestive juices in, and damaged the area round the orifice. All this had to be attended to, and the patient instructed in the care program. Some patients were so weak and feeble they never managed for themselves at all and how they got on at home is one of life's mysteries.

It was smelly and unpleasant work and I seemed to spend much of my day with poop.

A lot of the surgery was done for common conditions. Excision of anal warts or haemorrhoids . With the latter it was very important that constipation did not occur in the post-operative period and to ensure a good recovery we had to make every patient a jug of Senna tea. We would get dried Senna leaves and pour boiling water on them, the patient was expected to down the full jug every day. It was very effective even though they said it didn't taste very nice. It seemed that almost every locker on the Ward had a jug of this Senna tea on operations day. I never tasted it but must have prepared dozens of doses.

A young man arrived with a condition called pilonoidal sinus; this is where hair grows under the skin, on the Coccyx area (near the butt) and causes infection and an abscess. Young, hairy men were especially susceptible to this condition. Scheduled for surgery he was considered a 'dirty' case and was last on the operating list.

I had never seen this operation and treatment before, and two days after the event was told to go and clean and dress the wound. Again it was a packing job and yards of tube gauze was taken and the eusol and paraffin to soak it in.

The dressing was plastered down and when removed I was horrified to see that where the sinus had been excavated there was a hole big enough to put your fist in. It must have been horribly painful, but the young man was a complete stoic and barely flinched as I slowly cleansed and packed the wound. I had no idea that a' boil on the bum' could result in such extreme surgery. This man was on the Ward for over two weeks having dressings and still had a huge hole when he was finally discharged to the care of the District Nurse.

One lady called June came in with Crohn's disease. She was only in her mid twenties but was married and had a caring supportive family. She was in very poor shape and had been in to the Ward many times before and had her bowel resected on several occasions to relieve her condition. She now had an illeostomy and what little was left of the bowel had flared up again, and although she was on drug therapy, was not doing very well.

She was one of Rita's favourites who was constantly at her bedside whispering, and no doubt making bitchy remarks about all and sundry.

June was not happy when I attended her and I felt this was a result of her relationship with Rita. Sometimes I had to care for her as there was no one else to do it. She was in a terrible mess and going downhill fast. Eating was difficult for her and even a low residue diet set the condition off. One day when I did her ostomy I noticed that there was faecal fluid leaking out of an old wound on her abdomen. This was a very bad sign and due to her debilitated condition not much could be done to help.

Rita started shrieking about this as if it were the Nurse's fault. The Doctors decided against a return to Theatre as she was too ill and weak.

One day Rita spent all morning with her. No one was allowed near. Finally the bed curtains were drawn and an hour or so later Rita came out red-eyed as June had passed. There was nothing to be done. The cause of the illness was not known then as auto-immune disease had not been discovered. This is a vicious condition and although we have better drugs nowadays there can still be a poor outcome for persistent disease.

At the end of the Ward were four beds reserved for patients with liver failure. There were no transplants then and these men gradually starved to death.

All the patients were given an IV and TPN.(Total parenteral nutrition) this was a thick white fluid dripped in , which could be absorbed direct by the body and did not need the liver- in theory.

The men gradually went downhill and grew thinner and thinner. You got used to how they looked but I had a few days off after night duty and was shocked to see the state these men were in on my return as they looked like they were in Belsen Concentration camp.

Needless to say, one by one they died. It was upsetting but nothing could be done for them. None was an alcoholic and their liver disease had another cause. They were all under fifty and some had young families. What they were doing on a bowel Ward is unknown, but Hospice Care then was rare and their families could not cope with them.

I think Rita docked me days off whilst working as my time there seemed endless and I frequently worked ten days on the trot. I had one weekend free in the whole three months. The Ward Sisters had a lot of power and it was unlikely that this exploitation and overworking would be picked up by the Admin. No doubt Rita was aware of this.

My social life picked up. Bau was older than Chris and I and her 21st Birthday was due soon. To celebrate this, her parents came over to England and hired an Apartment in Bayswater.

This was actually a Council flat, rented and then sub-let by an Opera singer who was away on tour.
The accommodation was very luxurious and was stuffed full of antiques and valuable furniture.
Bau's mum was tiny, pretty and very beauty conscious. She had fantastic clothes and a mink and leopard skin coat. She brought a personal servant with her who did all the washing, cooking and housework and would sally forth shopping in London by bus and always tried to pay the penny fares in high denomination notes.
She was Oriental and exotic. She went to bed every night at 8pm to preserve her youth, and her face was caked in nourishing cream.
It was obvious that she was under pressure to keep herself attractive, for even though she had given her High Flyer husband four children, she had to compete with his Concubine and second family living in Hong Kong.
She spoke no English and we communicated with smiles and head nodding.
There were frequent meals out and I was included in the trips. We did the London Hilton, The Savoy and various top range Chinese restaurants. Wherever we went the best of everything was offered and Bau's dad would sit at the head of the table with a bottle of Whiskey. He never drank wine or other drinks but just loved his Johnny Walker Red label.
I had some great times out and frequently we would go to the Bayswater home and the personal servant would cook us a meal.
Bau's birthday was spent in a famous Chinese restaurant and was a memorable night out. She was given a huge diamond ring as a family gift and lots of other stuff as well.
I was amazed at this display of wealth. It was way out of my league but I was taken along for the ride and did not object.

At this time we discovered Vidal Sassoon's hair salon. First Bau had a fantastic cut and looked wonderful so I decided to go. I think it cost about a third of my months money but I was delighted with the result and just had to economise even further .
Now I was back in London I resumed my Agency work to earn extra cash.
Some of my jobs were very strange to say the least.
I was asked to go to a house in Kensington to care for three boys. It was a huge house and I was introduced to the boys whose ages ranged from nine to thirteen, by the regular housekeeper. The parents were not in evidence and I was asked to prepare egg and chips for tea. The boys were sullen and uncommunicative, so I just got on with the cooking. I had never made chips but knew how to and I just had to manage and produce a decent meal. The owner of these children was a major film star and his wife was well known on the silver screen too. Neither parent seemed to care that I was there, or bothered to ensure that the children were OK. I never saw either of them. The Housekeeper had left my pay in an envelope.

Whilst I was there I took a phone call from another well known Celebrity and he was conducting a clandestine affair with the wife.
Later it hit the papers and had I been interested could probably have spilt the beans and got a payment.
It was sad seeing the boys as they were obviously unloved. I explored the house which had about five floors and saw that most of the rooms were furnished with props from a film that the father had starred in.
Many years later I heard that the eldest boy had become a drug addict and overdosed, killing himself. The gross and obvious neglect of these children was sickening, but I saw a lot of this amongst wealthy people on my job experiences.

Another job I was given was to care for a little girl whilst the parents went away for the weekend.

The parents discussed their requirements by phone. They had a little girl aged just three years and would be away Friday night until the Sunday. I was to have sole charge and would I please come wearing my Nurses uniform?

This latter was not really allowed but I decided to do it anyway.

The family lived in Knightsbridge in a luxury Apartment and were American. I was not invited to meet my charge and turned up on the Friday night wondering what to expect. It was 6pm and the parents told me the child's name but nothing useful about her routine or preferences. It was as if it were someone else's child and they were not really bothered.

They said there was food in the fridge, grabbed their cases and shot out of the door. I had no contact numbers or idea where they had gone.

The poor little girl named Amy burst into tears at their departure. Here she was left alone with a complete stranger and I was beginning to wonder what I had let myself in for?

The crying and sobbing went on for over an hour. Amy never uttered a word to me throughout my stay. She looked upset and terrified.

There were no toys in the place and apart from her cot and pushchair no sign at all that a child lived there.

I inspected the kitchen and the food left turned out to be a meat loaf and nothing else. No cereal, eggs or anything. There was about half a pint of milk and this and the meatloaf was supposed to feed the two of us for the weekend. This was not uncommon with wealthy people who seldom catered in the home but ate out.

However it was very odd that with a child in the house there was hardly anything.

Amy and I had some meat loaf each for tea and at 8pm I settled her in her cot. She was obviously toilet trained but there was no potty so I had to sit her on the toilet which was much too big for her. She had stopped crying but looked frightened and lost. It was so sad and I felt that at the very least I should have had an introduction to Amy and not been dropped on her as a stranger. She was too young to understand that her parents were away for a short break and obviously thought she had been abandoned.

The next day we walked out with Amy in her pushchair, and I found a shop to buy bread, butter, cereal and more milk. I was annoyed at having to buy food as this should have all been provided.

We passed an uneasy day and although I chatted and even sang to the child she did not respond and was morose with downcast eyes.

Somehow we got through the day which was a big relief as the employers were due home on Sunday and I was feeling more and more uncomfortable with the situation.

The next morning I was woken to the sound of Amy crying and leapt out of bed to attend to her.

She had wet the bed and was terribly upset about it.

I chatted to her kindly and said it was an accident and she must not worry at all. I stripped her cot but could not find any sheets that fit. Eventually I had to fold a double sheet for her and put that in.

We finished the meat loaf for lunch but at least we had cereal for breakfast and bread when required. I made Amy tea and warm milk. She did eat but never said a word.

At about 7pm the parents returned. There were no kisses or greetings for Amy. She might as well not have existed. They paid me my fee and fares and wanted me out ASAP. I tried to explain about the wet sheet but they were not interested. I did not mention the food and

although I felt very sorry for the child was glad to distance myself from these cruel and hard hearted parents.
You do wonder what effect this sort of upbringing has on the child long-term. No doubt Amy would be packed off to Boarding school at the first opportunity so that the parents could continue their selfish lifestyle.

Mrs Bau was very pleasant to me and on one visit to the Bayswater flat presented a really glamorous evening top. It was white silk and encrusted with pearls. A beautiful garment, but my social life would not present an opportunity to wear it. I think Mrs Bau was worried about me as her oldest son Mark who lived in London, was taking a romantic interest. He was nice but that was it. I did not reciprocate his feelings and his mother observed the situation with concern.

Doris invited me to another Sunday lunch and Susan and baby Alex were staying. I took the evening top to show them, and Susan was very taken with it and asked me if I would swop it for an electric iron. I agreed to this as needed an iron and with all the Officers Mess parties and functions she attended it would get well used. The swop was done and I had no regrets as the iron was very useful and I could not have afforded one. About 18 months later Susan asked for the iron to be returned as she had virtually worn the top out, and it was now rather tatty. She said I could have it back! I could not believe her cheek and told her that I was keeping the iron and that was that! This was typical of Susan and her grasping attitude and how she tried to cheat all and sundry. She was incredibly thick skinned too, and even when spoken to rudely would not turn a hair!

I had another holiday and again decided to go home. Hilda and Reg had now moved to York and were living in Married Quarters at Acomb.
The house was warm and pleasant but we were crowded as Susan and the baby had turned up. Susan loved staying with other people, and would point out how much money she was saving on housekeeping by sponging off others.
We were both in the kitchen one day and had a disagreement on some trivial matter. Susan became hysterical and started throwing pots, pans and crockery at me. She smashed loads of stuff and was screaming out abuse. Hilda turned up and calmed her down. Nothing was said about the breakages and I don't think Hilda even asked her for the money. Hilda said that Alex was away for a long time and Susan was upset. Baby Alex witnessed this aggression and the poor little chap cried.
Susan was prone to these outbursts and I was told many years later when her divorce from Alex was finalised she smashed up all the furniture and ornaments in her Home.
The stay at Acomb was not really memorable except Hilda and Reg had several rows as Hilda was sick of the RAF and wanted Reg to resign. She also disliked Acomb and was looking to buy a property in York City.
It was nice to catch up with Margaret and Maxine and again we discussed how mean the lifestyle was with Hilda. The two girls had no winter coats and had to wear their school macs everywhere. Hilda would not buy them one although she had about ten coats herself. I couldn't help as had so little money but heard later that Reg had got involved in the debate and ordered Hilda to get them one each. This again had resulted in huge screaming matches, but Reg was adamant and Hilda had to part with some cash. I can't say I enjoyed these holidays much but we did have some fun and I would buy sweets and chocolates and share them with my sisters.

I continued on the Colostomy Ward and got very tired. Long days and working really hard took its toll and I was glad when my three month stint came to an end and again I was to get a break with two weeks in the Nurses school.

I was summonsed to Rita's office to get my Ward Report. It was very nasty and insulting. She didn't have a good word to say even though I felt that I had worked my socks off. I got upset and had a few tears as was so angry and frustrated. This woman was catty, unfair and destructive. I imagine if she liked you things would be fine as she could not down every one, but there was no doubt at all that I got the thick end of it.

I hoped never to see her again but as it turned out I did!

ANOTHER SCHOOL TRIP

This was our penultimate visit to the school and we were to learn more complex procedures. We were into our third year and were expected to take a lot of responsibility. Second down from a qualified Staff Nurse we worked independently and supervised other Nurses who were in earlier stages of training.

The School seemed like a holiday after my recent hard slog. It was interesting and a huge contrast with the PTS. Although most of us were only 20 years of age, we were hardened and experienced workers.

There was a lot of new stuff to take on board and we had lectures from some Senior Doctors. One lecture was about giving blood transfusions and the complications that might be encountered. Plasma, whole blood and packed cells were discussed along with storage and the importance of checking the blood for giving with the patient's notes to ensure that the Cross Matching was correct.

At the end of the lecture questions were invited. I wanted to know if someone had a cancer in situ and donated blood - could the disease be passed to a recipient? I felt this to be a reasonable query but the Doctor was not at all happy and shouted that nothing could be passed with the blood. He got really angry and seemed to take my question as a personal attack on his blood transfusion service.

Many years later with the onset of HIV, Hepatitis and CJD it was all too obvious that disease could be transmitted by this route.

Surely this doctor was aware and his denials resonated.

Another Doctor Lecturer was a Psychiatrist advising us about mainly Psychosis and the suffering of the afflicted. There was a film shown to back up her information that was very good but my main memory was of her chain smoking throughout her talk. She sat down for the lecture and had a lit cigarette going all the time. As one began to run out she would light up another. She must have smoked dozens a day. The dangers of smoking were not really recognised then but this addiction was the worst I had seen.

A lot of Medics and Nurses smoked and I would avoid the Nurses sitting room because of the grey fug smoking Nurses created. Even the attractions of 'Top of the Pops' on the communal TV were ignored because of this problem, and I imagine many of the Nurses experienced major health problems in later life due to the habit.

In school we learned about diabetes and the giving of insulin, also storage. Then Type 2 was unknown and it and Type1 were all lumped together. A lot of patients did not do their own injections and had a District Nurse out twice a day when at home. We were expected to do them in hospital. We were told about their special diet, and how sugar and too much carbohydrate caused a worsening of the condition. This illness was not very well controlled and the vast selection of drugs we have now had not been developed. The treatment seemed very haphazard and really only Type 1 diabetics got medication. Often we would find sugar in the urine when we did routine testing but unless the patient was at risk of a coma this was considered to be fine. Patients with advanced type 2 Diabetes would be admitted with gangrene following peripheral neuropathy yet still there would be no insulin given and the only treatment offered was amputation of the offending area.

Barrier Nursing and infectious disease was discussed and how to put on a pair of sterile gloves without contaminating them.
Often we gowned up to protect a patient from us, as by the 1960's many infectious scourges like TB were in decline. There were no known cases of HIV, and if you got blood on your hands from any source this did not cause alarm and was just washed off.
We had resistant bugs even then and most of the Nurses had seen gas gangrene in a wound and knew of deep seated hard to cure infections. Mostly we had an antibiotic that would work but over the years resistance to drugs has built up, and some infections are hard to get rid of.
We learned about giving eye drops, how to do a burns dressing and as if I didn't know? How to care for an ostomy.
We needed to learn how to catheterise a woman. This was frequently done by Nurses and in fact we should have been giving this on bedridden, incontinent patients as is done nowadays. Surely it's better to have this type of drain in, instead of lying in a wet bed and getting macerated buttocks and the development of pressure areas?
We did not do men and this was left to the Doctors. The reason given was the men having a longer urethra but as Nurses do it now I think it was to save men from being embarrassed.
More trolley laying - up was taught. This time for a Spinal tap for both investigation, and the diagnosis of stroke or meningitis. We now knew all manner of different trolleys and how to assist Doctors for a variety of procedures.
Many patients at the Westminster had cancer and received radiotherapy to the tumour site. Skin reactions would occur like severe sunburn as well as making patients feel ill and tired. We needed to put special cream on the affected area, and watch carefully for any tissue breakdown.

My mentor Tutor Sister Simpson, seemed to know about my bad report from the Bowel Ward and asked me about it. I stated my case that the Sister had taken against me, and even though I had worked hard and gave my best, she was determined to find fault. I pointed out the good reports I had on the Orthopaedic ward and Obstetric Unit and said I was upset and angry at Rita's unpleasant remarks. I think the Tutor was a bit surprised at my vehemence and let things drop.

Now we were Second Years we were told that we could 'Live-Out' of the Nurses Home in our own accommodation. Bau, Chris and I started a search. Money was a big problem for me and I could only afford a minimal rent. We decided to put an advertisement in the Newspaper to see if we could find something and after it ran we had two replies.
The first one visited was an absolute, vile slum. The man who took us round was a' spiv' and had no shame in showing us a disgusting room with the door hanging off. The decorative order was bad and the floor bare of carpet. Shared facilities revealed a filthy toilet and bath that appeared not to work. Horrified that people lived in such squalor we removed ourselves and the putative landlord drove off in his top marque Mercedes - Benz car.
The second property was better but occupied by two women. There was a very unpleasant smell in the place and fittings and furniture were minimal. The main problem was it was more than I could comfortably afford and a long trek to the Hospital. This then was a no-go as well.

The idea of living out was a problem. The truth was I simply could not afford it. Most Nurses parents paid rent for their daughters to enable them to have the independence of living away from the hospital but I never had a brass penny from home throughout my training.
Bau threw us a bombshell. Her dad had bought a Flat in Neasdon and it was to be ours to live in and we only had to pay a token rent. This amazing piece of information pleased and excited me. Getting away from the horrible Nurse's Home room was a priority and this was an offer almost too good to be true.
Shortly afterwards we moved to the flat. It was two bed - roomed and I had to share with Bau.
Although at the outset this seemed like a dream come true, the reality was that Neasdon was a very long way from the hospital and whether you made the journey by bus or the Tube it took well over an hour. It was fine while we worked short hours in the school, but once the long shifts clocked in the trip became onerous and exhausting.
There was a hill between the station and the Flat and on my early shift I was always late and would run up this hill to catch the Tube. On top of this I was eating less and began to lose weight. I didn't realise this but went into a dress shop and got into a smaller size frock which was happily bought. It was very pleasing. I also found a job locally doing some babysitting and this accumulated extra cash.

My 21st Birthday was coming up and as we were in the Flat we decided to hold a party. This generated a lot of excitement, and planning. I had noticed that on the bus coming home from work there was a very, nice cake shop in Brixton so one day I got off the bus and entered the shop to order myself a birthday cake. Invitations were sent out to various friends and we began to prepare food. Chris and her culinary skills was very helpful, and made a Cordon-Bleu liver pate. I paid for all the food and drink, and the day was eagerly anticipated.
On the day I collected my cake and by the evening we awaited the arrival of guests. I had a phone call from Geoff saying he couldn't come as he was at a wedding and could not get away. Several others also failed to turn up, but in spite of this we had a good time and a lot of hospital friends were there. The food and drink went down well and the cake was outstanding - really delicious, and worth every expensive penny.
Bau and Chris gave me a fitted, vanity case for my birthday, plus cards, and I had other gifts from party guests. Hilda sent me a horrible, cheap looking, red, nylon nightdress. Obviously one of her cast offs as it was worn and had no labels on it. She also sent a creepy card. It was a picture of a witch stirring a cauldron. I don't know where she got it from but it was the most unpleasant card I have ever seen. We had a phone in the Flat but there was no call from my parents and I decided not to ring them as was sick of their mean behaviour.
Bau and Chris asked what I had from home and I lied yet again and said that it was money. I hid the card as it was so embarrassing when compared to their nice ones. Still it was a good day and memorable and happy milestone.

The school was finishing and we all knew that the next visit would be a one week 'crammer' for our finals. The new Ward destinations were posted and I was to go back to the Vauxhall Hospital to work in the Operating Theatre.
I had heard mixed reports about this and knew I would be required to sleep over some nights at the Hospital to cover for emergency operations.

THE OPERATING THEATRE EXPERIENCE

There was a lot for me to learn about the Operating Theatre. I was the most junior member of staff and initially had to act as the 'Dirty Nurse' and remove waste and assist the Scrub Nurse (scrubbed up to assist the Surgeon) as needed. We had been taught in the school how to gown up and even though I was only the run-around I had to go through the full cleansing procedure which included washing hands for five minutes before putting surgical gloves on. A lot of very major surgery was done in this Hospital and the two Consultants had Bi-weekly lists for operations.

We had a great deal of bowel surgery. Sometimes both surgeons would work on a patient doing an AP excision, (Abdomino - perineal) for cancer of the rectum. A colostomy would be formed and the tumour excised. The rectum was removed and overall the operation took about five hours.

Each pack used was opened by me and in its internally sterile wrapper was offered to the Nurse. Swabs, sutures and small items were taken with sterile gloved hands and added to the piles of instruments already on the table. Every instrument and swab used was counted. Packs of ten items was standard and at the start and finish of each operation we counted them carefully. At the end of the operation, they were checked again to avoid leaving a foreign body in the patient. Sometimes we were a swab short and the Surgeon was told. He then had to fish about in a large bloody wound to try and find the missing item, locating lost swabs and instruments could be very time consuming but it had to be done.

We had wheeled bins for rubbish and these were not touched but kicked about as needed. One day a man had his leg amputated. It was pretty horrible listening to the surgical saw but finally the limb was severed. The scrub nurse handed the leg to me to get rid off and I nearly dropped it as it was so heavy. It was a thin leg and I could not believe it was such a weight. No matter what happened we were expected to cope.

There was general surgery done as well and I saw hernia repairs and appendectomies. Due to the amount of abdominal surgery done we had return patients for an operation called separation of adhesions. This was scar tissue that stuck onto inner organs, often the peritoneum and caused exceptional pain and distress. It seemed very common, and we had a lot of work from this complication.

All the time I was watching what was happening and saw how the Nurse assisting the Surgeon would display the instruments and thread up the needles with catgut for stitching the wounds.

She was busy and sometimes had to help expose the wound with retractors, and would also iodine swab the patient prior to an incision being made. It was repetitive work and I soon learned what was required with the different operations.

One day after three weeks or so the Sister in charge of the Theatre said I was to be the Scrub Nurse for a Hernia repair. I was very nervous even though I had seen the operation done several times.

Once you were gowned up and 'clean' you had to wait for help with obtaining materials for the operation and the Staff worked as a team for the best possible patient outcome.

I got through the hernia operation, handing the right instruments and threading up the stitch needles. All the swabs etc were accounted for and I realised it had gone well. I was sweating with fear and my gown was drenched. It was incredibly stressful that first time scrubbing up but as the weeks went by I did more and even got to help with an AP excision. My confidence rose and it all became quite enjoyable. I never minded seeing the operations except for the first incision. Once the body had been 'opened up' I was fine and also with the stitching of the wound, but the first cut was hard to look at.

Every Thursday I had to stay at the hospital in a sleepover room. It was very basic and there were no amenities whatsoever. It was typical of the Hospital that rated Nurses so low that they would provide such poor living accommodation. There was no bedside light and the bedding was inadequate. Such luxury as a radio was non-existent - far too good for lowly Nurses.

The only plus thing was the food and that was illicit too.

If the Surgeon was working late- and sometimes they did not finish until 8pm, the Hospital kitchen would send up a heated trolley of food. Mostly this went untouched as the Doctors and Nurses would want to get home and would shoot off. Because I was required to clear up the Theatre I took my pick of what was usually delicious food. There was always masses, but I don't think any of it was meant for me.

After an operation all the instruments were taken into a large duty room for cleaning. First they were scrubbed with detergent and then dipped in a liquid called lube to keep them in good working order. The cleaned items were rinsed, counted into packs of ten and put in the Autoclave in large metal containers. Most of the things were made of stainless steel and the instruments were put on a disinfected trolley when done and covered with sterile sheets to be wheeled back into the theatre.

I spent hours cleaning instruments and noticed that one of the Surgeons who was short and fat used small, stubby instruments. His opposite number who was tall and slim used long and thin equipment, and this was to do the same job.

There were all sorts of tools in the store room that were used and one thing that really made me shudder was a machine for slicing off skin for grafts. The store room looked like a torture chamber and some of the items were scary.

I seemed to do well on this Ward and the Sister was very nice to me. Sometimes Rita would appear with a patient from her Ward and I would glare at her as best I could from behind my mask and she would glare back. I think there was some animosity between her and the Theatre Sister as they never spoke and of course this removed the opportunity for Rita to blacken my name.

When my three months in Theatre ended the Ward Sister gave me an excellent report and invited me to go back and work there after I had taken my finals. I said I would think about it, but felt it was more a technician than Nursing job and was not attracted to a career there. It was ideal if you did not want to interact with patients.

I was finding the daily grind to Neasdon a huge burden. Frequently exhausted I would have a very prolonged bus trip to get home after Night Duty.

On top of that I was not getting on well with Bau. Another friend of Bau's called Liz had moved in and was sharing with Chris. I felt unable to cope with the travel and one day as I did my ironing and everyone was present I said that I could no longer do the daily journey and was going to move back into the Nurse's home.

This bombshell was received in utter silence and then to my great surprise Chris spoke up and said she had enough of the travelling as well and would be joining me. Bau looked furious and didn't say anything. Liz had a boyfriend and liked to see him from the flat so she was definitely going to stay. It was a shame but from Bau's reaction I realised that if I moved out our friendship was at an end.

The very next day I visited the Accommodation Warden and told her my tale of woe. I asked if there was any chance of going to another Nurses home called St George's House in Vincent Square right by the Nursing school. This place had a really good reputation.

Indeed there was a room available but it was a double and Chris and I would have to share if we moved in there. Having been used to this in the Flat we grabbed the chance with both hands, and within days were out of Neasden and back in SW1.

ANOTHER NEW WARD

My new Ward was a General Medical back in the Westminster and again there was a very nice Ward Sister called Margaret. She was quiet and calm and seemed to take everything in her stride. I was considered to be fairly senior now and to prove my merit was wearing a hat which we called a Frilly.

This came as an oval piece of highly, starched lace and you had to stitch it to make a little round cap with a pleated upturned tail. We were all proud of these hats and they marked you out as a Third Year.

The only difference in uniform now to a qualified SRN was that this rank gave you an Apron without straps. The Ward sister wore a dark blue dress unlike our denim. The uniform represented the Nursing hierarchy and we were all aware of each other's status by what we wore.

I don't think the patients were understanding of these subtle differences, and even in PTS I would get called Staff Nurse and even Sister!

It was easy to find your way round the Ward as they were all of the same design. A men's and women's Ward, and several rooms in the corridor for either patients that needed quiet or who were private and paying for their bed.

We had two cubicles on the general Ward as well and very sick people went into these where there was privacy, peace, and yet constant surveillance by the Nursing staff.

Every day food was sent onto the Ward by the Hospital kitchen. Patients had a cooked breakfast plus cereal or porridge, and then a hot main meal at midday. There were menus to be filled in every day, and those on special diets were catered for. These were many and varied. Low residue, puréed, diabetic, obesity, coeliac and religious. The list was endless and each patient was matched with their needs and little named containers would arrive for them.

In the evening high tea was served at about 5.30pm and on top of this there was afternoon tea and a late night drink.

The nurses dished up and gave out the food. In this way each patient got appropriate nutrition and we could see if anyone was not eating, or had a dietary problem.

Some old and frail people had to be fed and as a senior I could avoid this as it was one of my most disliked jobs. It was always the poor First Year that got the task of trying to get food down patients who slobbered and spat and in many cases did not want to feed at all.

One lady in-patient claimed to be a vegetarian. She was very picky and although the kitchen sent her nutmeat croquettes, cheese pasties and other fare she always left everything. She complained bitterly about the food and we all felt exasperated by her fussiness.

One evening on a Sunday (many patients had been discharged) , salad was sent to the Ward in a huge metal container- enough for at least a dozen people, and it was all spare. I was in charge of the meal wagon and a vegetarian meal was sent to the woman. It was instantly returned and I felt annoyed. When I had finished distributing the other meals I picked up the whole serving dish of salad, took it to her and said sarcastically, "here's some salad for you. Do help yourself!"

I walked off and later to my amazement saw she had eaten all of this huge amount of vegetation.

"Thank you Nurse-that's the only decent meal I've had in a week" she said. I was speechless and removed the empty container.

Another patient came in. She was a relation of the Consultant and got into a private cubicle as a perk.

She had cancer and again refused the food that we served. For a cancer patient this was worrying and I tried to persuade her to eat." I'm too ill Nurse "was her reply to my encouragement, and another full plate was returned.

Every night this lady would have visitors and they always drew her curtain, I supposed to have some privacy. One evening for some reason I went behind these curtains and to my surprise saw the woman who couldn't eat slurping down a big portion of very buttery asparagus. There was crusty bread and cooked chicken breast on her locker too. She was having a feast and I realised that this went on every night and I was worrying needlessly.

The Hospital was really a small community and if anything happened the news soon got round.
A celebrity patient, a scandal, or something funny, especially from Casualty. One night one of the Sisters came round carrying a jar.
"You must look at this" she said.
In the jar were three large, red worms. Pretty much like what you dug up in your garden. She told me that these worms had been coughed up by a patient from the Middle East and were a parasite. They were truly disgusting and made me feel sick. After her visit I think every Ward in the hospital got to see the worms, and it certainly made one think about the risks of overseas travel.
Another story that circulated was about a man who took some drug that must have been similar to Viagra. We never found out what it was, but he had a huge erection that would not go away and became very painful. According to the rumour he was admitted to Casualty where he ran about yelling and shouting, and no one could help him. In time- about six hours the effect wore off but this was considered to be highly amusing by everyone and I heard the story several times.

One thing I disliked doing was arranging flowers that friends and family brought in. They were a nuisance and took up valuable time. As well as this they all had to be carried out the Ward at night. I decided that I had enough of flower arranging and when a bunch arrived, I would go to the sluice, get a vase and water and smiling nicely ask the flower bringer to arrange them. This worked well usually and in fact it gave visitors something to do. What was irritating was that the visitor would ask to borrow my scissors. Now these were carefully guarded as high pilfering of such went on. The pair I bought prior to Nursing went in about two days. If I did not remember to pick up the scissors as soon as the flower arranging was complete they would disappear. It was annoying. I no longer purchased scissors but would retain a pair from a dressing pack, but always felt guilty doing this. The scissors just seemed to vanish into thin air.

Everything was a learning curve and the longer I had on duty the more confident I became in managing anything that was either disliked or to be avoided.
This included feeding patients, getting bedpans and emptying commodes. In spite of this I did have more than my share of these when I was a junior.
I have a very good sense of smell and this is not an asset for Nursing. The cancers smelt foul, pneumonia had a peculiar ' maggoty' odour and you could smell blood after operations. A lot of infected dressings had an offensive niff, and on top of that was stale wee, especially in catheter bags, and the inevitable incontinent poopers.

One of the patients was quite young and had come in for investigation of a bowel problem. Nothing was found and she was all set for discharge. Suddenly her temperature peaked and she said she was in terrible pain and could not go home. She was referred to the Houseman who after examination could find nothing wrong, but her temperature remained up and she kept groaning, sighing and holding her tummy.

After a few days of this the general consensus amongst the Nurses was that she was malingering and for some unknown reason did not want to go home. One of the Nurses said that her temperature was always up when hot drinks were served and we began to wonder if she was dipping the thermometer to appear more ill.

More days passed and her moaning and groaning increased. It was decided to have her examined by the Registrar, and this was duly done. Far from saying she was a fraud he diagnosed acute appendicitis and arranged for immediate surgery. She was rushed to theatre as an emergency and we were told that her appendix was on the verge of perforating. Had this occurred it would have been a life threatening situation.

We were all red faced about this. None of us had taken the woman seriously and as such we were all guilty of a degree of negligence.

The Ward Sister gave us a lecture about the situation and I think we all learned something by the experience.

We had a very old and poorly lady admitted to the Ward. It was obvious that she did not have long to live. It was rumoured that her son was a senior Doctor in the Hospital and she was very poor and had worked as a Char Lady (cleaner) to put her son through medical school. He repaid this sacrifice by distancing himself from her and in the few days she had as a patient he never once visited or came near.

I was on Night duty and during the shift this lady passed. She had been in a coma for two days so it was no surprise. The Night Sister attended and phoned the Doctor son and told him that his mother had died. He still did not visit.

At about 5 am the phone rang and it was the son. He asked me to go and take off his mother's wedding ring and put it in an envelope for him to collect the next day. I was outraged. Apart from anything else all possessions of the deceased had to be listed and taken to the mortuary with the body. I told the Doctor this and said I would not get the ring. It was a bad situation and this man seemed to be totally callous and uncaring about his mother. It was very sad to see that this poor woman had been abandoned in her time of need and the only interest shown was in the ring.

Chris and I settled into our shared room in St George's House. It was L shaped and so we enjoyed a considerable degree of privacy.

Once in bed we could not see each other and as we mainly worked opposite shifts, mostly we had the room to ourselves.

I was a bit worried about Chris. She was a depressive and was frequently very withdrawn. She was secretive too and did not communicate very well or discuss how she was or even what was happening at work. Another thing that concerned me was that she had helped herself to drugs from the Ward - mostly Barbiturates, and had dozens of them stored up in a large, glass jar.

At the time these drugs were commonly used. Every patient was offered night sedation to help sleep on the noisy Ward. This was standard and the drug of choice was usually Butobarbitone but there was a whole selection and Chris had all of them from the looks of things.

St George's House was much better than Queen Mary's . The room was nicely furnished and had carpets and electric points to play our appliances. On the landing there was a kitchen, well stocked with tea, coffee and milk, plus bread, butter, a toaster and various jams and spreads. Total luxury compared to all the previous accommodation.

We could have breakfast too, and the leftovers were sent to the kitchen and platters of sausage, egg and bacon arrived most days which I really appreciated.

It was such a relief not to have the long Neasden journey anymore but Bau was out of our lives and I only ever saw her in the Nurses school and she was not speaking.

Susan had another baby even though Alex was only just two at the time. It was a little girl and now she was seven months old I was asked if I would visit and babysit the two kids so she and Alex could get a break for the weekend.

They were now living near Lincoln in a rural area and I went to the station to get a ticket. To my amazement the woman at the ticketing office said she had never heard of Lincoln, and she had to do a major search to find the ticket.

When I arrived at Susan's house she gave me a quick run-down of the baby's routine and also how to care for Alex; told me there was food in the fridge and then disappeared.

My niece and nephew took to me quite well to say they had hardly ever seen me before and I did the baby's feeds and settled her and sorted Alex out. The baby was very large and weighed about 22 or so pounds and I found the weight onerous in general handling.

The next day was a Saturday and having got the children up, washed and fed decided to do a trip to the shops. All the lifting and handling was exhausting and the whole situation was very hard work.

Alex had a little bike and wanted to ride this to the shops, and foolishly I agreed he could. On top of the kids there was a dog called Sally (A Border Collie) and she needed looking after and exercising as well.

We set off with the baby in the pram and Alex peddling along on his bike. I had the dog on the lead. The shops were about a mile away and all went well at first. After a bit Alex decided to go it alone and shot off into the distance on his bike. I shouted for him to come back but he completely ignored me. The dog was not happy about the situation and pulled off the lead and ran after Alex barking. Frantically Sally tried to round the runaway up and kept circling us, doing her best to keep the 'flock' together. I was worried sick that I would lose Alex and finally our dysfunctional unit reached the shops. No sign of my nephew or the bike.

Sally was still barking and just as I was starting to panic, Alex came merrily peddling along and clearly did not understand why I was shouting at him.

By Sunday I was exhausted. I had no idea that caring for children was so tiring. The baby Lucy was very good and as long as you shovelled plenty of food in she slept all night and seemed contented and happy.

On the Last morning I nosed round the house and noticed a cut glass decanter with some drink in it. The stopper was immovable and although I didn't like spirits was determined to taste it. I went to the kitchen and got a damp cloth and pulled hard, twisting the stopper. After a few attempts I managed to pull it off and smelt whiskey which I didn't like and forgot all about the project.

Later Susan told me that this was an antique Decanter and Alex senior had been unable to remove the stopper for fear of shattering it. The Decanter had been to two jewellers who had also said removal of the stopper was risky and declined the task. My inquisitiveness had really paid off!

But I could have risked a big bill for myself if things had gone wrong.

Susan and Alex returned in the evening and I stayed until the Monday as I was on 'nights off'. I was glad she was back as I was tired out. She never said where she had been and I had no reward for my efforts and even got no refund of the fare there!

3 Susan, Alex Junior and Annette(on right) on a day out.

Christmas came again and once more I was working. Not only that
but I was also on duty over New Year.
Again most of the patients were discharged and we were told we could work whatever hours we liked. My preference would have been none, but I showed up at 11am and realised there was nothing much happening. For some reason I felt really upset to be on duty and didn't like the hospital's idea of celebrating this special time. We had a choir on the Ward and a lot of the Nurses had tinsel in their hats and most seemed to be loving it.
We had our lunch in the Nurses dining room and it was nothing special.
As only the really ill patients remained on the Ward working seemed to be in almost total silence. A few visitors turned up but apart from that it was boring. More staff came on in the afternoon so at 6pm I left and went back to the home.
I phoned Hilda and Reg, and again I did not get to speak to my sisters but heard that a wonderful time had been enjoyed, chez Brown and this made me feel worse. As I was paying for the call I did not stay talking long and had an early night not really appreciating my working Christmas.
Chris was off for the holiday and had flown home to Ireland, she did not return until after the New Year so was very fortunate.

One of the patients who had remained in over the holiday was a man from Indonesia with Buergers Disease. This is where the peripheral arteries close down and in his case this was caused by cigarette smoking. He had gangrene of the foot, had lost several toes and only had about two fingers left. In spite of this and advice from the Doctors he persisted with his smoking habit. He would balance a cigarette between the stumps of his fingers and inhale. There was a constant smoky, fug around his bed but in spite of warnings, admonishments and encouragement he would not stop smoking. He was now scheduled for amputation of his foot but did not seem bothered. He really was a warning against the dangers of smoking and it went to show that if people were determined to kill themselves it was difficult to stop them.
Another patient came in and we were told she had terminal cancer of the breast and it was just care and kindness required.

I was scheduled to do her bed bath with another nurse and after we took her nightdress off came eye to eye with the cancer. It was a shocking sight. A huge red mass, that looked like volcanic lava, spreading from her left breast to across her neck and half way down her back. Not only that but it was rock hard and truly evil looking. It made your eyes water to look at such a horrible sight.

We helped the lady as much as we could, and completed the bed bath putting on talcum powder and cologne to mask the smell of the huge tumour. She was very stoic about her condition and just accepted it. No mastectomy had been done so it was probable she had not sought help for her condition until it was far too late. Afterwards, I said to the other Nurse that I had never seen such a bad case of cancer, and wondered about the woman's prognosis with such advanced disease. Usually people died long before this stage was reached.

"The last time I saw cancer like that the patient was dead in two days" said the other nurse. These words proved to be prophetic and sure enough the poor lady passed two days later. The odd thing was she never complained of any pain and declined the analgesics offered and all the standard cancer relief.

Another patient was admitted. She was only 23 years of age and seemed happy and bouncy. I clerked her in with the usual process and asked what her diagnosis was. "Its Malignant Melanoma" she told me. I had never heard of this and she pointed to her knee and leg. There were three, small black moles visible and this was the Melanoma.

The Sister told me that the woman- Janey, had a very poor prognosis - the Melanoma visible was like an iceberg, with the main problem underneath and hidden from view. The fact was this young woman was riddled with a terminal cancer and had a very short life ahead of her. It was hard to believe as she seemed so well and yet a couple of days later I heard on morning duty that Janey had passed away in the night. It was totally incredible that a disease which manifested as three, small black moles was a deadly killer.

CHRIS DICES WITH DEATH

Chris had fallen on her feet with her Ward and was on the private Maternity Unit at the Westminster.

She came back with tales of screaming women, multiple, elective Caesarians and flowing champagne. Security on the Ward was very tight and although I had visited in the hope of seeing the new babies, the place was locked up and curtained and there was nothing on display. There were no NHS Maternity beds in the Westminster but other London Hospitals located nearbye could offer this service to patients.

Chris really enjoyed her placement and patients celebrating the births were very generous. As well as boxes of chocolates, Chris was given vouchers for Harrods and Fortnums plus opportunities to obtain free theatre tickets.

It really was a case of being in the right place at the right time and if anything should have cheered her up this was it.

However, one morning I returned from night duty at about 8.30 am, and as I entered the room saw she was asleep in her bed. The next moment she sat up and vomited violently. Her vomit was a mass of pills, the Barbiturates that she had been stashing away.

I rushed forward and spoke to her. I should have called an ambulance as she could have digested more, but I knew if I did this she would get the sack for thieving drugs off the Ward. I simply didn't know what to do. Turn her in or take a chance on her being OK? I checked her pulse which was steady and her eyes seemed normal with no pupil fixation. She crashed back into the bed and slept. I monitored her for about an hour and everything seemed normal. I cleared up the mess she had made and after three hours of observing her with all seeming

well, I went to bed myself. I was taking a huge risk doing this and was lucky that she survived.
The next day I saw her and she would not discuss what had happened but the jar of drugs vanished and I hoped this was an end to this sort of behaviour.
Many years later she did pass after 'inhaling vomit' leaving behind two little children of her own and three step-children. She had received a lot of psychiatric care in the interim but all to no avail. One of her treatments as a psychiatric patient was sleep therapy and she was drugged for days to achieve this. She was thrilled to bits at the time as she lost a lot of weight, but this treatment was banned later as it became known that those treated became suicidal.
She was dogged by the cruel disease of depression and finally and very sadly it took her life.

I started the Agency work again and did a few more jobs.
The first was a family in Kensington where I was required to care for the children. It was again an odd set up with three kids aged 9, 6 and 3 years - a girl and two boys. The mother was there but didn't seem interested in her children and I was to amuse them. Again there were no toys but the little girl had a pet mouse that she carried about. The three year old curled himself round my legs and refused to walk, so I spent the whole time carrying him and he was very heavy. It was all a bit surreal but when we got to 5 pm the mother asked me to make some tea. I had to point out this was not possible without a shopping trip as the fridge and larder were totally empty.
Un- phased she said we would eat out later. This was hardly satisfactory for young children and when I was dismissed at 7 pm they still had no food and nor had I.
I was glad to get away as found sharing the lifestyle of this family to be unpleasant and the mother seemed to be on another planet. Recreational drugs come to mind but I will never know.

Another Nanny job took me miles on the Tube, all the way to Wembley. It was again a childcare job and I was to have sole-charge while the mother went out.
When I got to Wembley I had a long walk to a mean little house in an even meaner street. The door was opened for me by a thin, anxious looking woman. "Thank goodness you've come" she said. "I have urgent business with my Solicitor".
She explained that her husband had left her and she was going to try and get maintenance payments for herself and the children.
I then met the children who were all black. Obviously the mother had been married to an African and the children had nothing of her apparent in their appearance; you would not have guessed they were mixed race by looking at them.
The children were terrified of me and all four of them ran and hid behind the sofa. The mother left and I was just a minder and had no interaction with the kids whatsoever. I tried talking to them and being friendly, but they ignored me. They were all aged under 6 years and due to social attitudes at the time I imagine they had no support or interaction with neighbours.
It was a very long afternoon but I suppose no one came to harm with my presence and after four hours the mother returned.
"Thank you" she said, "You can go now".
I told her my costs plus the fare. She said that she owed me nothing as had paid the Agency. In fact there was a joining fee to the Agency of about £30 to cover unlimited staff bookings for a year and this rather ignorant woman though that she could have as many Staff as she liked free by paying this sum.
I had to explain that my fee was in addition to the Agency charge and her retort was that she had no money and couldn't pay me.

My fare alone had cost me nearly a £1. After explaining this she agreed to pay the fare but I didn't get a penny for the four hours work, and two hours travel.//
I did ring the Agency about this but it was no skin off their nose and they were not interested. It was all rather unpleasant, and I did feel sorry for the woman as divorce and abandonment were uncommon happenings.

Chris had impacted Wisdom teeth. Her face swelled up and she seemed to be in terrible pain. She got herself admitted to the Nurses Care Ward and enjoyed the full package of pampering that was on offer. I visited her a few times and was most impressed at the coddling and sympathy given to the in-patients.
Chris swanned about in a negligee and eventually got scheduled for surgery. She would have the offending teeth removed under General Anaesthetic on The ENT Ward.
I visited her the day after her surgery. She was back with the Nurses and told me she had stitches in her mouth. Her face was swollen and she looked like a hamster. She was pretty poorly for a few days, but finally perked up and told me that the Sister there had liked her so much that had requested she work there and when she had finished the Maternity Ward that was where she would go.
I could only attribute this huge bonus to 'the luck of the Irish'.
This placement was much coveted and was probably the best job in the hospital for a student Nurse. In one way I was relieved as felt that a stressful placement might bring her down and back to another overdose.

I continued with my own Ward and got to Nurse a man with PVS. (persistent vegatative state)
Because resuscitation was not often successful this type of patient was unusual.
He lay in bed and had a catheter in and an IV. He was tube fed and totally dependent on Nursing care.
He was washed daily and cleaned after episodes of incontinence of faeces. He lay in the bed and his eyes were open and although he moved his head about, did not respond to any stimuli or talking.
Basically he was a vegetable. He was only young- in his early twenties and it was all very upsetting.
Bau had been on this Ward and told me about him. She was all for letting him die by removing his drip and the feed tube. I never saw a relative visit so it seemed that no one cared.
I suppose that where there's life there's hope but this case could go on for years as long as the basics were attended to. Tony the patient was still on the Ward after my three month placement.

Another sad case was with a young lad who had been in a motorbike accident in Spain. He had broken limbs and a severe head injury. His initial treatment was in Spain and was very poor.
His broken legs had not been set properly and his skin was crusty and scaly from neglect.
His parents had visited Spain to be with him but seeing how bad his treatment was had him medevacced back to the UK.
He was conscious but not really with it and kept saying "no, no" when spoken to.
His limbs had to be re- broken and reset and intensive physiotherapy was instituted. A Speech therapist visited and a full care operation commenced.
I witnessed three months of this treatment and saw a massive improvement in the lad. By the time I left the ward he could answer simple questions and was walking by himself with a

Zimmer frame. The intensive rehabilitation continued. His parents visited every day and were delighted with his progress. It really was as if he had been brought back from the dead.
I heard that after about six months he was walking and talking almost normally and went home into his parents care. It may be the case that he got to go out to work again as such a massive improvement was achieved.

One of my last experiences on this Ward was nursing a very nice American lady. She was one of those special people you occasionally meet who has an aura of goodness and peace around them. It was a pleasure to help her in any way possible and she always had a kind word to share.
We all knew she had terminal cancer and was dying, but she did not seem to be in much pain and was always cheerful and positive.
One night duty I found her awake at Midnight and made her a milky drink. We had a little whispered chat and she settled down. At about 3am, I returned to check if she was alright, and saw that she was lying on her side smiling. She had passed. She looked happy and peaceful, and my first thought was that she had seen heaven. As I thought this I heard the hymn 'All things bright and beautiful' playing in my head ,and even in death this wonderful lady had brought spiritual upliftment.
I shall never forget her. She was a beautiful person.
My time on the Ward ended and I had yet another holiday.

MORE MISTAKES

Some months earlier I had summonsed up courage to go and visit Nanny Lou.
I knew this was a big taboo and if Hilda learned of the visit I would be cast out of the family for good.
I got a bus from Westminster that went all the way to Hackney as I knew the address. It was a long ride and my courage started to flag. We reached Dalston where my Uncle John had an Off-licence and on the spur of the moment I jumped off the bus and visited him instead.
I didn't get the big welcome. He was busy in the shop and having said hello and given me a bar of chocolate showed me the door.
All my resolve to see Nanny Lou vanished and I crossed the road and caught the bus home.
I have always regretted this. I would have reconnected with a much loved grandma and would have gained a lot by permanent separation from my parents - but it was not to be.
I never saw her again and also lost contact with my Uncle Bill through this. Lou would have accommodated me for holidays and so with hindsight realised that not visiting on that day was a big mistake.
As I had another two weeks holiday I went to York where Hilda had now moved to and was living in Bootham just outside the City wall.
I finished a 1-9 and went to Euston station on a bus and caught the last train to York.
The train was empty and it was dark and spooky on board. As I was wearing my Nurse's cloak and uniform the Guard decided to keep an eye on me and kept visiting to ensure that all was well. It was long after Midnight when I arrived and Reg did pick me up, which must have been a nuisance to him.
Hilda had got a bargain with the house which had been bought off two old ladies. For peanuts she had acquired most of the furniture as they were entering a Nursing Home.
It was top quality furniture and the house was spacious and centrally heated. Amazing standards for Hilda and Reg, and very comfortable compared to the RAF places.

There were three bedrooms and I shared with Margaret which was great as we could have long private conversations at night whilst in bed. A lot of this was about our parents and their horrible ways. We got on very well. I didn't have a lot of time for Maxine who was immature and very much under Hilda's influence.

Having so little money that most of the time was spent in the house.

I went to a Spiritualist church one afternoon, with Hilda and she got a message from the Medium. This was all about how wonderful she was and what a high spiritual place she occupied ,and her great talent for communicating with the Spirit world . It made me realise what a fraud this so called religion was. Hilda was a money-worshipping, cold-hearted Psychopath, and if her 'Spirits' thought otherwise it raised big questions about them!

Hilda was determined to get Reg out of the military. She nagged on and on, having occasional bouts of hysterics to strengthen her case and gradually she wore Reg down.
The fact was she could not upgrade herself to the Officer lifestyle. Reg had done well turning himself into a Flight Lieutenant from a Cockney boy who left school at 11. He really was a rags to riches example, and on top of that he loved the RAF life. He had moved smoothly into management and adopted all the norms required.

Hilda was small minded and selfish. She did not care that she was ruining Reg's life and career and could only ever think about herself. She seemed to mesmerise him, and with her constant rows and nagging usually got what she wanted.

Hilda was always very class conscious. She denigrated anyone she considered socially beneath her calling them 'Working Class'. Certainly Nanny Lou and all of Reg's family fell into this category, and for this reason Hilda wanted nothing to do with them. Now she was an officers wife she was automatically given higher class status, but the fact was she could not cope with this and had a terrible inferiority complex. She could not deal with other Officers wives who were educated and articulate and was paranoid about them. For this reason she wanted Reg to leave the RAF

After I returned to London I heard that Reg had resigned his commission and was applying to go into the Civil Service.

THE CLOCK IS TICKING TOWARDS OUR FINALS

We went to the Nursing school for a last week and this was the Crammer for our finals. We were given projects to work on as we would need to do a written paper and also have a 'Viva 'and be expected to give a practical demonstration of our skills.

We were told that a patient was to be admitted with pneumonia and had to get the bed and likely equipment ready. This was quite easy as we all had relevant experience. One group of Nurses got a bit carried away, and with a case of TMI (too much information), decided that the patient should be admitted into' postural drainage'. This was a rarely done procedure and had to be ordered by the doctor. To make a very sick and weak patient lie upside down in the bed was laughable, and it was lucky they did not do this stupid action during the Finals Viva. They would certainly have failed and been viewed as a danger to patients.

We got quizzed about drugs and blood tests and although I knew most of the medicines given on the Ward again, having no reference book was a worry.
Crash trolleys were relatively new entities and all the elements were discussed and we were given further instruction on resuscitation. In fact unless we were first on scene there was usually no role for the Nurse other than running with the trolley. We all felt ready for our finals and we had indeed come a long way from our first time in this place of learning. My main worry was about drugs. I could not afford the £3.50 required for the necessary textbook and only knew what I had learned on the Wards. I did manage to borrow a book but was really concerned not to have my own for reference. I had a Nursing procedures book, Anatomy and Physiology for Nurses and a medical dictionary which were very helpful, and used these for study and revision. Notes had been taken in the school and these too were useful.

BACK TO WHERE I STARTED

We all got to chose where we wanted to work and I opted to go back to my first Ward the ENT.
I was now on the brink of being qualified and was given much more responsibility.
When the Sister went off duty I was often the Senior Nurse left in charge. The keys to the drug cupboard would be given and with a junior I would do the drug round. It was required that responsibility was taken for all manner of injections and IV's including Blood transfusions.
On night duty I covered for three wards and would be asked to give dangerous drugs, check drips and attend to any patient that was giving cause for concern. All this for about £15 per month!
A Night Sister patrolled the Hospital and would come onto the Ward to inspect. She would expect me to know the name and diagnosis of every patient-all 40 of them. Even if I had been off for a few days and this was a first shift. It was ridiculous and any ignorance was reprimanded.
I found that if I knew the long stay patients, which she did as well ,I could invent names and conditions for the rest. I was never rumbled but what really irked was that even visiting another ward on a request, she still expected me to know all the patients. On the three Wards this added up to over 120 patients and unless you were brain of Britain with a photographic memory, impossible.
I enjoyed the Nursing now. The menial jobs were done by the first and second years and I seldom gave a bedpan.
It was expected to give Bedbaths for the very ill, and even the Sister got involved with this sometimes.
I did dressings of surgical wounds and removed sutures and clips. On Operation days I would give the pre-meds (relaxing shots prior to surgery) and frequently escort patients to the theatre. Once back on the Ward they would be checked for vital signs, and pain relief given as needed. This was often more shots and I was pretty skilled at giving injections.
 A lot of teaching went on and juniors had to be supervised with new to them, tasks and procedures, and admonishments given for poor work. Life was busy and time flew by at work.

There was another third year on the Ward called Rosemary. She should have been qualified but had failed her finals and was waiting to do a retake. In theory she was senior to me but the reality was we were on an even keel.

She was very sweet and charming, but was bone idle. There was nothing she liked more than getting into the Office after the Sister had gone home, and entertaining the Houseman with a tray of tea and biscuits. Rosemary would sit chatting and enjoying herself whilst I did all the work.

One day we had a lot of surgery patients needing care, plus we were on take from Casualty. A lady came in who needed catheterising and I was so busy with drugs and other things asked her to do it. Her face fell and she said " I've never done that-I can't catheterise".

I was really shocked. It was obvious that this girl had been skiving throughout her training and could not perform a basic procedure. No wonder she had failed her finals.

I handed her the drug keys and went off to do it myself. She was not fit to be a Staff Nurse and if she had anything about her, at the very least she would have asked me to show her the technique.

About a week later she told me that the Matron had asked her to represent the Nurses at a garden party for the Hospital held in the House of Commons and would I partner her. We were to sell roses at some extortionate price and dress up as old fashioned Nurses.

Apart from the fact I looked and felt extremely fat, my shoes were disintegrating and I could not afford a new pair. My bank account now had a £5 overdraft and monthly charges were made. Effectively this presented a choice of living on £10 one month or remaining in debt. In spite of my tatty shoes I said it sounded attractive and agreed to go. Hopefully the long dress would cover the shoes.

It was amusing that this idle, incompetent Nurse had been chosen to represent the Hospital. She was pretty and always immaculate. Her apron was pristine as she never worked to soil it. To all appearances she was a perfect role model, and even Sister McLeod had failed to rumble her. I really could not understand how she got away with it?

We went to the House of Commons dressed up in old fashioned Nurse's outfits for the Garden Party. It was busy and we sold single roses at two shillings and sixpence each, but it was for the Hospital charity and we did a roaring trade. All went well until suddenly we were accosted by an old lady. She clearly had a grudge against Nurses and decided to take it out on us. She shook her fist and screeched and shouted at us. This caused a commotion which was exactly what the old woman wanted. She went on for about five minutes and neither Rosemary or I knew what to do. She clearly had mental health issues and was getting more and more aggressive. Suddenly two security guards turned up and physically dragged our assailant away. The last we heard were more squawks and shouts as she was put outside. One of the guards came back and asked if we were OK? He added that the woman was a regular there and a pathological attention seeker.

This certainly spoiled what would have been an enjoyable afternoon, but we had sold out of roses and decided to go home.

Because I was so short of money I telephoned the Agency again for more work in my days off. I asked if there was other work as the Nannying was so problematical.

"Could I cook?, would I be prepared to help with table waiting?" was their response, and my reply was yes.

Now cooking was a bit ambitious as my skills were somewhat limited to nursery food and fry ups, and I had never waited on table before but was willing to give these challenges a go.

A job was offered in the Bishop's Avenue in N2. It's probably the most expensive real estate road in the whole of the UK but I had no knowledge of this when I went to help with a dinner party.

The house was stunning. It was modern and had a floodlit lake in the garden. The owners who were giving the dinner were a young couple and the wife was in a late stage of pregnancy.

All the guests arrived bearing gifts for the baby, and there were heaps of packages and I was expected to dispose of the wrappings.

The dinner table was set and there were two cooks in the kitchen.

With the 20 or so, guests sitting down the meal started. There was asparagus in butter and I duly took these to the diners, working along with another staff from the Agency. This gourmet dish was followed by roast partridge and all the trimmings, and I was rushing about serving and clearing. All went well and we reached the pudding course which consisted of some creamy confection.

We cleared up afterwards and suddenly our work was over. The cooks were to wash up and it was time to leave this hive of luxury and go home.

The pregnant wife paid us our due and asked me if I would come again in a couple of weeks? I agreed this, but about three days later she phoned me and cancelled. It was a very odd call and she seemed to think her cancellation had broken my heart. The truth was I couldn't care less, and thanked her for the call. She kept saying over and over that she didn't want to upset me. I assured her she hadn't but she kept repeating herself and asking if I was alright? It was quite exasperating and she would not accept that we should both move on and finish the call. It was all rather strange and I felt there was some other agenda here but had no idea what it was or what she wanted.

The money paid was better than the Nannying and I was able to buy a pair of cheap shoes for work, as the old pair were split and broken down. This was a big relief because I had noticed the Sister staring at my feet with distaste.

Another Agency offer presented. Could I do a dinner party? I assented on the basis that it was nothing complicated and was referred to the client.

A couple of days later I went to meet my employers and view the menu.

Far from being basic this was Cordon-Bleu.

Avocado soup, roast pheasant with game chips and bean sprouts, and fresh orange and crushed, caramel pudding.

I went home and told Chris. She collapsed laughing and said even with her training she would find the meal difficult and she despaired of me coping.

"What are game chips?" I asked. She explained but said you needed a 'mandolin' kitchen appliance to make them and potato crisps would do instead. She really was none too helpful and just thought the whole thing was hilarious.

On my return to the menu the meal had been started. My employer had made the avocado soup, added cream and was slowly heating it up. Asked for my opinion I felt it was bland in flavour and needed salt. A tiny bit was added that made no difference and now it was time to prepare the oranges. Each one had to be cut in half and each segment removed. I had never done this before and found it very messy and time consuming. After a very long time the dish was ready to have the crushed caramel spread on it. I boiled the sugar and water but it would not set. It took for ever, and finally started to burn. I whipped it off the stove and turned it onto a metal tray. Once cooled it could be crushed. The pheasant were already slow- roasting and just needed basting and the bean sprouts were washed and ready for cooking. It was agreed I would come back at 6pm to get the meal completed.

I returned and was now on my own. A server turned up- also from the agency, and it was up to me to get the meal on the table.

I had no idea that the bean sprouts needed only light steaming and dumped the lot in a huge pan of boiling water.

The meal started and there were 16 eaters. The soup was sent in and now I had to halve 8 pheasants, plate them up with the crisps, and drain and put on a portion of the soggy bean sprouts. The meal was not a huge success, and I was relieved to serve the pudding and know the dinner was at an end.

I don't think the employer was very thrilled with my efforts, and was hostile and very reluctant to pay me. It was a small, hourly fee and he should have been employing a proper, professional cook for his sophisticated menu and not sourcing someone at the cheap Agency rate. However this was my first and last cooking job and I stuck to waiting at table from then on.

I had only one more waiting job. This was for a huge dinner for over 100 people. It was served in a large hall and was easy to distribute, and I got to help with the pudding preparation. This resulted in me slurping down a lot of chocolate sauce.

It was good fun and there were five of us from the Agency. When we had finished serving we were allowed to eat up the leftovers and this evening was a big success, not to mention getting good pay. I wished that the serving and waiting had been a first job choice because the Nannying was a hard slog and paid really badly.

Because we were nearing our finals I started looking at post-graduate training options and the thing that seemed to offer the best pay was Health Visiting. In particular there was an advertisement in the Nursing press for students on incredibly attractive training packages in a previously unheard of place called Rotherham.

This offered a one year college training, with full pay- equivalent to a Sisters salary; rent paid as a student, plus all textbooks spending refunded. On top of this any interview expenses would be paid. It was a dream come true and both Chris and I sent for application forms. Having duly submitted these, two weeks later we were on the train to Rotherham for our interviews.

We passed Sheffield and entered a landscape of coal pits and slag heaps. It was dreadful and as the view deteriorated we started laughing. It was so awful we could not believe it, and in fact it still did not sink in that the attractive offer advertised masked the fact that this was a very deprived area, and working in such would be extremely challenging.

Our interviews went smoothly, and we were refunded our fares and given a meals allowance. This went down very well, and the interview had been conducted in a highly professional manner. All the signs were good. We were told that our years training would be done at Sheffield Polytechnic, with practical work and clinics worked in Rotherham.

The money and perks were amazing after London, and both of us decided to accept the offer that was made to us to start that September. There was an option to start in the following year so we could do a year for the hospital, but both of us had enough of the Westminster and wanted out.

Time was moving fast. Our finals were approaching and I spent a lot of my free time studying. A great deal was learned on the Wards, especially about drugs and new procedures. I think everyone was worried about the' Viva ' as we knew this was the part of the exam process that was really testing. Having a face to face question session would be difficult and you had no idea what you would be asked about.

The clock ticked and in spite of our approaching trial we were worked as hard as ever with long exhausting hours.

I was working on night duty and not sleeping very well. The constant changes of working days and then night played havoc with bio-rhythms, and left you feeling drained and exhausted.

I decided that I would wait until the end of the night duty and take a sleeping tablet acquired from the Ward. I got two Mogadon (Nitrazepam) and having got myself ready to sleep settled in my room at 9am, thinking I would sleep in until about 6pm. The two tablets were far too big a dose but as I saw loads of patients taking this amount, I didn't hesitate.

I woke up and it was 8pm on the clock. I felt a bit disorientated after the 'Moggies', but was alert enough to notice there was something odd about the light. The sun should have been going down, but it appeared to be rising in the sky. I looked out of my room and it was quiet but I did spot one of the maids with a laundry basket. Slowly it dawned that it was not evening but morning and I had slept 23 hours. That was the first and last time I ever took a sleeping tablet, as somehow a whole day had been lost. Not only that I had a headache and felt hung-over. Thank goodness I had not taken the drugs with a work schedule or would have failed to make it.

Chris was now working on the Nurse's Ward and having a good time. The duties were light and there were lots of extras to be had like afternoon tea with the Sister and an option to eat on the Ward instead of going to the Nurses dining room.

I met more difficult patients on the ENT Ward and one was a drug addict.
These addictions to Heroin were not common at the time and I had no experience in this area. The man was only about my own age and was whining and demanding. He had come in for a Nasal Polypectomy which is minor surgery and should have been a one night job. Somehow he managed to stay on and was whinging and demanding. He was having methadone syrup to try and wean him off the addiction and if he was refused a demand, would say he would not take his methadone. Some of his demands were outrageous. "Would a Nurse come and sit with him?"As if we could spare someone for this! "Could he be taken out for a walk in a wheelchair?". As soon as you said no, he started making threats.
"I'm not taking my methadone "he said when I refused the walk. Exasperated I was really rude to him.
"So what? - I don't care whether you take it or not", I replied. This did not go down well and the man said he would report me. I never heard anything more and he was discharged the next day. It put me right off drug addicts and it was hard to understand how someone could waste their life on heroin? I wondered if the drug made him so unpleasant or he had always been totally selfish?
We had two Staff Nurses on the Ward. One was tall and slim and very good at her job. She was completing her year for the hospital and was leaving to go and become an Air Hostess for BOAC. She was a huge loss to the medical profession ,but the long hours and poor pay were the reasons for a mass exit of qualified staff and she told me that after four years work she was completely 'burnt out', and couldn't wait to leave.
The other Staff Nurse was Welsh and was very thin and hyperactive. Her main topic of conversation was about her boyfriend who was a Doctor.
According to her I too should find a medic as she would be enjoying the good life with her marriage, and I needed to get on board. She constantly pointed out the advantages of her lifestyle and encouraged me to link up with a medical student at the very least.
She was bossy and tended to tell you things already known. One night we had to put up a blood transfusion and I was to accompany her, collect the blood in a glass bottle from the duty room fridge, and check the patient's notes for blood group, cross matching. Having done the necessary we set off for the patient with her carrying the bottle. "Don't ever rush "she said, as she tore along. Suddenly she lost her balance and went flying. She dropped the blood and the Bottle smashed on the floor. A pint of blood goes a long way and the mess was terrible. With her eyes bulging and gibbering with agitation she told me to go away and she would sort it out. I was pleased to leave this gory mess and it must have taken her ages to mop it up. Also she would have to report the breakage and this would not have been well received.
She improved in her attitude after this loss of face and became easier to get on with.

I did a week of nights and this was tough.
As well as looking after the ENT Ward I was expected to be the Senior Nurse for two other Wards as well and it was a lot of responsibility.
One night the Hospital Admin sent a qualified Agency Nurse onto the Ward and she took over the senior role. She was from the Caribbean and not very communicative. She did the drug round and then disappeared. I was busy as we had post-operative patients who needed a lot of care.
It got to about 2am and I was ready to go for my meal but the Agency Nurse was nowhere to be seen. I guessed she had been called to one of the other Wards, but I could not leave for my meal until she gave me the go-ahead.
One of the patients was incontinent and I needed to change the bed. As I opened the laundry room door, to get some fresh linen, I found the Agency nurse had taken two chairs in and was sound asleep. It was well known that some of these Nurses 'moonlighted', working day and night shifts. This woman wanted the money but was shirking.
I should have called the Night Sister and reported her, but instead shook her awake and said that when I had settled my patient I was going for my meal. This was agreed and I set off.
When I came back from the meal she was nowhere to be seen, and after a look round, found her again fast asleep, back in the laundry room. There was no point whatsoever in employing her.
All she did was the night and morning drug round, and slept the rest of the time.
The Hospital had to resort to Agency Nurses as there was such a shortage of trained staff. It was rumoured that these Nurses earned £7 per night, as against my £15 per month.
Sometimes when on the 1 to 9 pm shift there would be no senior or qualified Nurse to take over from me and I would have to phone the Nursing Administration and ask for relief.
Frequently it was 11pm or later when someone came and of course I did not get a penny for my overtime
One night I did not get off duty until after Midnight and had to get up for a 6.45am start the next morning. I overslept and was ten minutes late getting on duty.
The Assistant Matron (the Martinet) saw me going on duty late and had me to her office and gave me a dressing down about my tardiness. I tried to explain but she wasn't interested. It all seemed grossly unfair and it was this sort of attitude towards Nurses welfare that really irked.

A couple of nights later when I was doing the drug round I was shocked by a boy of about 14 who was in for a tonsillectomy. He was post-operative and when he saw me with the drugs came running up and asked for "some blues". I asked him what he meant and then realised he wanted a dose of phenobarbitone. How he knew about this drug was beyond me, but obviously where he came from these barbiturates were common currency.

It was surprising the number of Nurses who left after a year or so and then returned from a six month break. There was no regard for their years training and they had to go back to PTS and start all over again
One such person was a girl called Elaine . She had started in my set and then had a year out after doing 22 months training. She was now a First Year again, as I was preparing to take my finals. She said she had been unable to settle outside of Nursing and requested to come back.
I admired her because it must have been very hard to go to the beginning and start all over.
Another Nurse called Cherry had a terrible case of Acne. Treatment was poor with no drug therapy, and her only help was to have radiotherapy to her face. She had no choice with this and was told by the Nursing administration that she was an infection risk and if she didn't have treatment she would be asked to leave.
It was a terrible affliction for a young girl anyway and even worse to lose your job over it.

The treatment she had was effective, and when I next saw her although she still had scarring to her face, the open, suppurating spots had cleared up.

THE FINAL EXAMINATIONS LOOM UP

Time marched on and the final SRN examination approached.
Once I told the Sister the dates in June, she gave me two days off before, so that I could do some last minute revision.
The examination was in two parts - written papers, and the 'Viva', where we wore uniform and had the practical examination.
First came the practical, which was held in a demonstration room in the Wolfson School of Nursing. I was teamed up with another Nurse who I had never met or seen before. Not a familiar face from my set. We entered the room and there were two elderly Nurses there wearing Sister's uniforms. One was sweet and kind and the other caustic, demanding and negative.
Our first task was to work together and get ready for an unknown, diagnosis admission to the Ward. My companion seemed very nervous and quiet, so I tended to take control and lead. We put out all the appropriate equipment for admission and then each of us was taken aside and asked about what we had done and the reasoning. I had the nasty nurse but felt on top of this question and gave a flood of information. When this was done she took me to one side, looked in my 'Yellow Book' and said that as I had done the Obstetric course I was to tell her about feeding a baby. I then noticed a lady in the room who was to be my' patient'. A dummy doll was given to her and I blathered on about baby feeding. I omitted to say much to the woman and addressed my remarks to the examiner. I got told off about this, but felt I had covered most things in my response.
Next we swopped examiner and I was put with the nice Sister. She smiled sweetly and said- "Come over to the drugs trolley Nurse and tell me all about them". My heart sank- this was exactly what I had been dreading.
I saw at once that all the drugs were familiar ones from the Ward and was able to rattle through them, including usage, dosage and potential side effects and contra-indications. We came to a sleeping drug used mainly for the elderly. It was called 'Weldorm'.
"What's the derivative of this drug?" asked the examiner. I had to think. The proper name was dichlorophenazine and I suddenly realised it was another form of chloral- a sedative mainly used for children. I offered this and the lady seemed delighted. "Well done Nurse'" she said and I instantly relaxed and saw that my worst possible fear had come to nothing.
Suddenly it was all over and we were dismissed. My cohort and I left the room not speaking and I never saw her again.
Sometime later I saw Sister Simpson and she asked how I had got on? I told her that it was stressful and gave the detail. "How was the other Nurse?" She asked.
"Fine I said, but like me nervous".
Sister Simpson smiled. "She was put with you deliberately as you have a lot of self confidence. She has previously failed her finals twice, and this is her last chance".
I knew you only got three chances at the exam, but thought it a bit of a cheek to put me with someone who could not cope. Still it was water under the bridge and I was glad I did not have this information at the time.
The Written Paper was three days later, also held in the School. First there were short questions and then we had to choose from five topics to write three essays on particular medical/ nursing subjects.

Having read the questions I realised there was in fact no choice as I could only answer three questions. The rest of the stuff had simply not been covered. So much for our 'top notch' education!

I was not happy about this and should have complained to the school. However Chris who had worked on a ward relevant to one of the questions could do the answers so I put the situation down to bad luck.

A BITTER ENDING

As soon as we had taken our finals Chris said she was going back home to Ireland as like me she disliked London and the Hospital and wanted out. Always inventive she wrote a long letter to the Matron saying that her mother had TB of the spine and she was going home to nurse and care for her. A total pack of lies, but Chris got the sympathy card from the Matron's office and left in a cloud of glory.

This all happened very suddenly. We did not get our SRN results until August and Chris was gone by mid-June.

I felt very lonely. Chris was my only friend now, and apart from my Ward colleagues I saw and spoke to no-one. On top of that, I had a letter from the Warden at St George's House asking me to vacate the double room, and I would have to return to St Mary's Nurse's home as there were no single rooms currently available.

Needless to say the horrible old room was given to me yet again and it was back to a very degraded, standard of living.

Generally the off - duty Nurses were not friendly and even in the dining room when you sat next to someone they would not talk. I began to feel depressed.

The idea of spending another year in this state was a heart sinker, and I decided to give in my notice as well. This was risky because if I failed my finals would have had to beg the Hospital to take me back. However the thought of staying on in the current circumstances overrode that and the letter was duly sent to the Matron.

I received a summons to see the Assistant Matron, the Martinet.

She was very cross with me and went on about the Health Visitor training as Rotherham had written for references. She said I needed a lot more experience to do the training and should stay on and complete a year, working for the hospital.

This lecture went on for a long time but I was not swayed. The loneliness of my position was the deciding factor and really this was my own fault for not joining in social opportunities and being slobbish and lazy in my off-duty.

I had to work out a final month on the Ward which would take me to late July.

I know the Sister was disappointed that I was leaving and as there was such a shortage of trained staff she might struggle to find a replacement.

At the end of July I went to the Nurse's sitting room and watched the Americans land on the moon. This iconic event seemed to underline how institutionalised I had become, because in spite of the hype it all seemed meaningless.

Things did not go well in my last week. I was assigned to Night Duty and although the general work was fine a man was admitted to the Ward who had severe psychiatric problems.

We were short staffed and he kept threatening to hang himself in the bathroom, and also took to threatening bed-bound patients. The Men's Ward was in uproar, and it became impossible to do normal work including the drug round in the morning.

I gave the report to Sister McCleod and told her about this man's disruptive antics. She said she would report the situation to the Doctors, but the outcome of this was that nothing was done and I had him again to manage the following night.

He didn't seem to sleep and was in and out of bed, shouting and upsetting everyone. Patients were woken up and the severely ill were frightened. The man needed urgent transfer to the psychiatric hospital, and we simply could not cope with him.

After a dreadful night as I was bed bathing a very sick patient the Junior Nurse ran to fetch me to say that this man was in the bathroom and was trying to hang himself from the toilet with his dressing gown cord. I had to drop everything and spend time trying to persuade him to stop what he was doing and go back to his bed. This took over half an hour and by the time the Day staff came on I hadn't even finished the drug round.

In spite of complaints from me nothing was done.

I had two more nights prior to leaving. My case was in my room so I packed it up, phoned the Nursing administration and said I was sick with gastric flu, and left the Nurses Home and headed off to York.

I was tired, exasperated and it was a sad end to my Hospital career. It was certainly not the end I wanted but was so demoralised I felt there was no choice.

It was an odd journey home. While walking along the platform to get on the train I slipped on an oil slick. My pink, cotton, best dress was covered in oil and muck and I felt like bursting into tears.

A nice lady came to my rescue and was very sympathetic. She asked me to accompany her onto the train and we ended up in a First Class carriage. I told the woman my ticket was for second class but she insisted I stayed and said she would sort everything.

When the Guard came to do a ticket inspection she had a word with him but did not pay a bean and he seemed quite happy for me to remain.

The lady told me she was a Spiritualist Medium and was going to some Stately home up north to do a seance and readings. She said I was not to worry as I would meet a nice young man, get married and have two children- A boy and a girl. Maybe this was guesswork, but it was spot on and these things did come to pass.

When I reached York it was early evening and Reg turned up to collect me from the station. I had no job and no money. It was another week before my results of the SRN exam came, and until I had this and a positive result there was nothing to do but wait. Once the qualification was confirmed Nursing Agency work could be obtained, but in the meantime I was unemployed and had an overdraft at the bank.

That weekend we had a bad experience. The York House was located close to the City football club and on the Saturday there was a home match. We had just finished lunch and vacated the dining room when we heard a loud crash and breaking of glass.

One of the football fans had decided to lob a brick through our window and was long gone by the time Reg ran outside.

There was a terrible mess with glass all over the table and chairs. Hilda had an attack of hysterics until Reg said the insurance would pay for the repair. We had brown paper at the window that night. It was very worrying but our road was a walking route to the football ground and some of the supporters were bad tempered yobs.

I got more and more worried about my result. What if I failed? What if the Hospital refused to have me back?

It was awful, but finally the day of the results arrived and I decided to telephone and pretend I was Hilda. I thought if it was me phoning there might be abuse and demands that I return to London.
I got permission to use the phone and made the call.
Having introduced myself I asked for the result.
Magic words were uttered.
"She's through she's passed the exam and is now a qualified Nurse.
I stuttered my thanks and put down the phone feeling elated. It was the best possible news and the future was fantastic.
Two days later a written notification arrived and it was time to move on and contact the York Nursing Agency.
Three gruelling years as Student Nurse were over and the feeling of relief was great.
I had been worked very hard and financially exploited by an uncaring Hospital Management and a Government that set low wages, and could not care a jot about how Nurses fared.
A couple of years after I left due to pressure in the Press a report was done on our wages and conditions and changes made. It was too late for me, and I was made to suffer post-Victorian standards, and had a very hard time.
The SRN was a great qualification. There were so many opportunities for a trained Nurse that I was spoilt for choice. I have never regretted my training, but once was enough!

End.

Glossary of terms

Houseman-junior doctor. In his first year.

Senior Houseman. -junior doctor in his second year

Registrar
Experienced doctor who had a lot of training and was usually in a speciality.

Senior Registrar
Senior Doctor who was high up in his specialist subject.

Consultant
Expert doctor in a particular field. Head of the Doctors team. There was also a Senior Consultant and this tended to be on a professorial unit.

Ward Sister
Senior Nurse who was in charge of a Ward and had a Nursing and administrative role.

Staff Nurse
A trained Nurse who was second in command to the sister. Each Ward had two or three of these.

Matron
Head Nurse of the whole hospital Group. Mainly administrative and leadership role.

Char Lady
A cleaner doing rough work in mostly private households. Was considered as one of the lowest grades of worker.

Gas Gangrene
A severe infection caused by anaerobic organisms called Clostridium welchii

Analgesic
Remedy to relieve pain

Yellow Book
A record of practical instruction and experience for the certificate of General Nursing. This book was issued by the General Nursing Council for England and Wales. It was carried to each Ward by the Student Nurse to record her experience and was signed off by the Ward Sister.

Scrumpy
Fermented apple juice. A Non-fizzy cider.

Squash
A fruit cordial that was diluted with water.

Mac
A raincoat

Printed in Great Britain
by Amazon